Jesuit Relations
The Documentary Relations of the Southwest

Rules and Precepts
of the
Jesuit Missions
of
Northwestern New Spain

CHARLES W. POLZER

D0772357

THE UNIVERSITY OF ARIZONA PRESS
Tucson, Arizona

About the Author . . .

CHARLES W. POLZER, S.J., a native Californian, has dedicated years to the study of the greater Southwest. Trained professionally in philosophy, theology, history, and anthropology, he enjoys a useful combination of disciplines to delve into Southwestern studies. He has published widely on the life of Padre Eusebio Kino, the seventeenth-century Jesuit missionary in the Pimería Alta, and was instrumental in the discovery of Kino's grave in 1966. A founder and the associate director of the Southwestern Mission Research Center, Fr. Polzer in 1972 was named ethnohistorian of the Arizona State Museum in Tucson.

THE UNIVERSITY OF ARIZONA PRESS

BX 3712
.A1 P64

I. S. B. N. 0-8165-0488-1 paper
I. S. B. N. 0-8165-0551-9 cloth
L.C. No. 75-8456

To the Blackrobes of the northwestern frontier
who lived by these rules
and worked for a better day
this book is humbly dedicated

Rules and Precepts
of the
Jesuit Missions
of
Northwestern New Spain

The Documentary Relations of the Southwest

This volume is one in a series entitled The Documentary Relations of the Southwest, *which includes three major categories:*

> *The Jesuit Relations of the Southwest,*
> *The Franciscan Relations of the Southwest,*
> *The Civil-Military Relations of the Southwest.*

These three divisions reflect the primary sources of documents for Southwestern history and ethnohistory. By their very nature they provide geographical, chronological, and topical control for the rich and complex resources in Southwestern studies.

Contents

Maps

Illustrations

A Word From the Author

This publication, *Rules and Precepts of the Jesuit Missions,* is one of a series of studies from the University of Arizona Press — The Documentary Relations of the Southwest. The basic premise of the series is that the scholar, the student, and the interested reader need a reliable source of information unimpaired by interpretive synthesis. Authorities in many disciplines have discovered the rich resources of Spanish and Mexican archives; anthropologists, medical researchers, and environmentalists — not just historians — are using these invaluable records. Unfortunately, however, the newcomer is overwhelmed by the complexity, extent, and disorganization of the data. This documentary series will provide a framework from which the scholar and the *aficionado* can more successfully delve into archival resources.

This particular volume on the Jesuit missions of Northwestern New Spain focuses on the administration of the mission system. The rules and precepts presented here should dispel the erroneous assumption of several decades that the frontier missionary was a free agent or that the mission was a mini-parish in the making. The missionaries labored under a highly restrictive set of regulations and legal requirements. Although the missions flourished at great distances from the capitals of political power, they were intimately woven into the fabric of religious and civil control. As these rules demonstrate, even the number of mules in a pack train and the amount of alms to a beggar were carefully and continually regulated.

If the Jesuit missions were so minutely regulated, it would seem that versions of these rules would be encountered frequently. The opposite, however, has been the case. The rules and precepts as presented in this volume were translated originally from a typescript copy that forms a part of the Roman Archives of the Society of Jesus. These rules and precepts had been reconstituted from a number of archival sources by the Reverend Gerard Decorme, S.J., of the Mexican Province. As noted in Part II of this study the major portions of these rules and precepts were found in a collection that had been recorded at the mission rectorate of San Francisco Borja in Sonora. Later research revealed that the original documents have become a part of the Archivo Histórico de Hacienda in Mexico City. Whether Father Decorme consulted this archive to compile the Roman typescript or whether the documents found their way to the archive at a later time has not been established.

Whoever reads this volume should keep in mind that rules do not describe history. They are guidelines of policy and conduct. At one and the same time they denote probable conformity and possible disregard. But in any case these rules had to be reckoned with as they affected life on the mission frontier. Their publication today will not touch our lives, but they should influence our interpretation of mission history.

CHARLES W. POLZER, S.J.

Acknowledgments

The research for this volume was initially made possible by a Graduate Fellowship from the University of Arizona. The Roman phase of the study was greatly aided by Ernest J. Burrus, S.J., friend and colleague in the Jesuit Historical Institute. Much encouragement came from the late Dr. Russell C. Ewing, Head of the Department of History at the University of Arizona. And the author can hardly forget his debt to the scores of forgotten missionaries who faithfully kept these rules.

Part I

Interpretation

*The facade of San Ignacio de Onavas, 1975. Although the nave has disap-
peared, a small chapel in the rear still preserves some of the grandeur of this
seventeenth century Jesuit mission.*

Terminology and Origins

When Herbert Eugene Bolton described the mission as a frontier institution, he considered it a pioneer agency which theoretically would have vanished with the advance of civilization. To Bolton's mind the mission was designed as a temporary phase of frontier development which, like a presidial garrison, would disappear after the political, social, and economic changes eliminated the need for the institution. As the agency which introduced indigenous peoples to the practice of the Roman Catholic faith, the mission would dissolve and transfer the care of the faithful to an established, secular clergy under the immediate jurisdiction of the bishops. But, as Bolton implied in mentioning the advent of secularization, the missions were not so easily dispensed with. Once established, although the geographic frontier moved leagues onward, the mission remained in the "interior" as a center for religious formation and directed culture change. These processes advanced much less rapidly than territorial conquest and simple admission into the Church. Eventually the missions did give way to the more routine institutions of the Church and society, but not before they were formed into a complex and minutely governed system.[1]

The present study does not intend to analyze the mission as a frontier institution or as a participating agency in the social organization of the frontier. This has been well achieved in previous investigations.[2] The object of the present study is to review the inner workings of the missions as a system, to describe and evaluate the more important methods employed by the missionaries, and to demonstrate the evolving complexity of the institutional mission. Historiographically this study accepts the findings of Bolton in regard to the mission as a frontier institution in the Spanish-American colonies and strives to deepen our knowledge about how that mission system operated.

The phrase "mission system" is employed to stress various interrelationships: between the missions themselves; their administrative organization

---

[1] Herbert Eugene Bolton, "The Mission as a Frontier Institution in the Spanish-American Colonies," *American Historical Review*, Volume XXIII (October, 1917), pp. 42-61.

[2] The bibliography of mission literature is extensive. Several important works concern northwestern New Spain and would be pertinent. Cf. John Francis Bannon, *Missionary Frontier in Sonora, 1620–1687*; Herbert Eugene Bolton, *The Rim of Christendom: A Biography of Eusebio Francisco Kino, Pacific Coast Pioneer*; P. Gerard Decorme, *La Obra de los Jesuitas Mexicanos*; John Augustine Donohue, *After Kino: Jesuit Missions in Northwestern New Spain, 1711–1767*; Peter Masten Dunne, *Andrés Pérez de Ribas, Early Jesuit Missions in the Tarahumara*, and *Pioneer Jesuits in Northern Mexico*.

and dependency on other segments of colonial expansion in New Spain; and their relationship to the other apostolates of the religious order that controlled them. Hence, the primary concern of the present study is not with missionary expansion or with the personalities who influenced that expansion. Rather, it concerns the nature of mission organization and methodology as it evolved from the somewhat simple commitments for conversion to a complex system that attempted to modify Indian cultures as well as inculcate new religious beliefs. This particular study is limited to the missions of the Society of Jesus in northwestern New Spain during the colonial epoch. Similar studies for other regions or other religious orders would be useful and valuable, but the research requirements together with the final synthesis would necessitate more space and time than is reasonably available.[3]

The literature of the history of missions is filled with commonplace terms. Although a discussion of these terms risks being superfluous, many of them have more precise meanings in their documentary context than normally accorded in historical literature.

The idea of "mission" is radical to Christianity itself. In any locale or era a Christian mission would denote a group or group-supported center, even if the center consists of a single person, in a religiously alien area. The whole object of a mission is its role of religious conversion which may or may not involve some degree of cultural change. The term "mission" is the nounal form of the past participle of the Latin *mittere*, which has the same overall meaning as the Greek *apostolein*, "to send." As a group of persons, a mission refers to those who have been sent by the Church on a work of conversion. As a place name, mission denotes the area in which proselytic activities have been undertaken; it also commonly refers to the residence of the missionaries themselves.

In the literature of mission history the context usually clarifies the particular connotation of "mission" being employed. While Europe was predominantly Catholic, or at least Christian, during the ages of discovery and conquest, the term *misión* was often applied to a group of men who were being sent from Europe to the New World to lead the barbarous peoples back to God. The Roman concept of religion was so deeply engrained in the thinking of churchmen and the general populace that the modern historian tends to accept these terms at face value without probing into the subtle variations of meaning. For example, the modern translator of a mission document commonly translates *conversión* as mission, but the original documents frequently distinguish between the two.

The stress which can be seen in misión is usually on the "sent" quality of the activity; it connotes an isolation, a physical separation and some sort of dependence on a group external to the area where the misión is located. Although the two terms, misión and conversión, are nearly synonymous, the stress of conversión is on the actual activity of a change in belief and subsequent cultural practices. A misión might be for several years hardly more than an outpost of example for people who refuse to accept the basic teach-

---

[3] Cf. Hubert Howe Bancroft, *History of the North Mexican States and Texas*, Vol. I, p. vii. Bancroft calls the northern sector of Mexico the preeminent mission field of America and suggests "the system" may best be studied here.

ings of the missionaries. The use of the term misión need not imply effectiveness or success. Conversión, however, usually connotes a process of acceptance and change. When the terms are used interchangeably in a document, the connotative quality of conversión is usually controlling the intended meaning of misión. But the exclusion of the term conversión in a document can lead to the suspicion that progress in conversion was minimal. As a matter of fact, the acceptance of Christian beliefs by the Indians of northwestern New Spain would seldom allow anything but a nearly synonymous use of the term. However, some misiones among Indian tribes never reached a point of conversion.[4]

The concept of a mission remained valid until the people in the surrounding region embraced the faith and adapted to the Spanish forms of political and social organization. As the initial states of converting the tribes were accomplished, the conversión gradually became more commonly described as a *doctrina*. "Doctrina" has a more precise and legal meaning; the *Recopilación de las Leyes de Indias* devotes whole sections to the doctrina.[5] The *Recopilación* clearly distinguished the doctrina from a *parroquia* which had the customary feudal connotation of a limited geographical area under the care of a *cura*, or pastor, who watched over the faithful in that area. The operative assumption of a parish was that the faithful were already fully formed Christians and full fledged members of the Church. The doctrina, on the other hand, presumed only that the area was inhabited by people who had accepted the faith, but were not fully formed in it.

The role of the mission at this stage of development was basically educational. Because the mission in any of its first three developmental stages (that is, simple presence, *conversión*, or doctrinal formation) had still not achieved its final goal and because the faithful in the mission region were considered neophytes, the mission remained exempt from many forms of taxation, especially from the *diezmos* or ecclesiastical tithes. These exemptions, which were prolonged in the case of several mission regions, occasioned much tension between the secular and religious clergy. An inspection of the historical documentation from the missionary epic will readily disclose the continual and intense argumentation over the problem of exemption from the tithe. To defend the exemption of the missions, the religious clergy, who championed the cause of continuing the missions, constantly reverted to the argument that the missions functioned as doctrinas and not parroquias.[6]

---

[4] Misiones were attempted among the Moqui and Apache. Father Luis Velarde, S.J., filed a report outlining an *entrada* into Moqui land as early as 1716. Cf. Letter of transmittal, Bishop Pedro Tapís to the Council of the Indies, *Archivo General de Indias, Audiencia de Guadalajara* (hereafter cited AGI, *Guad.*), 67-4-22; also recorded in the Pastell's Collection, Mexico, Vol. XXIV, p. 26.

[5] Cf. *Recopilación de Leyes de Indias, Titulo 13, Libro I*, in twenty-six laws or articles. See also Rafael Gómez Hoyos, *La Iglesia de America en Las Leyes de Indias*, Part III, pp. 155-224.

[6] Cf. *Tanto [Si]mple de Informe a S.M. sobre las doctrinas de las Indias.* Unpublished manuscript book; author anonymous; circa 1640. 91 folio pages located in the *Archivo Histórico de Hacienda, Ramo Temporalidades, Legajo 282, expediente 1* (hereafter cited AHH, *Temp.*). See also *Executas* of the Audiencia of Mexico, 1596, and a reply of the Viceroy de la Laguna to Father Bernardo Pardo, 1682, stating his doubts that the Bishop of Durango can apply *diezmos* to the missions. AHH, Temp. 324, expedientes 1, 4, 6, 7.

Although Spanish law recognized a "mission" as a distinct category, it normally dealt with the phenomenon in terms of the doctrina or the *reducción*.[7] The doctrina was truly fundamental to the operation of the Patronato Real in the New World, particularly as it applied to missionary expansion.[8] As long as the misión retained its status as a doctrina, the minister of the doctrina retained his salary, which was technically an alms, from the Royal Treasury; the people retained their exemptions and privileges.

Mission history often characterizes the coming of secularization as the onslaught of an acquisitive, civil society; more commonly the missions were under attack by the ecclesiastical hierarchy rather than the agents of the state. The King and Courts were far more willing to accept the pleas of the Fathers for their Indian flocks than to acquiesce to the claims of the Bishops who seemed to envision the riches of their dioceses as extending to the Straits of Anian.[9]

While a priest had charge of a doctrina, he held the position of a *ministro de doctrina* or *doctrinero*. By simple association with normal church-community vocabulary, a doctrinero might be loosely called a *cura*, or pastor. Mission regulations, however, insisted that the missionary whenever acting in an official capacity, such as signing baptismal registers, marriage books, or in official correspondence, should employ the title of the "minister of doctrine."[10] Both the religious and secular clergy were able to hold such positions, but the seculars acted as doctrineros with far less frequency. The religious clergy considered the position closely in accord with their religious institutes especially as it related to poverty and obedience.[11] True, the doctrinero had a steady income from the Patronato Real, but this was not enough to attract the secular clergy who were not bound by vows of poverty and were more inclined to build up strong parishes independent of the royal treasury.[12]

The *Recopilación de las Leyes de Indias* treats of another form of Indian community often synonymous with the organization of the mission; this is

---

[7] *Recopilación, Titulo* 13, *Libro* I, and *Titulo* 3, *Libro* III.

[8] See above, note 6; also, Nancy M. Farriss, *Crown and Clergy in Colonial Mexico, 1759–1821: The Crisis of Ecclesiastical Privilege.*

[9] See an unsigned draft letter with marginal notations from the archives of the Father Procurator of the Province of New Spain, Jan. 10, 1701; AHH, *Temp.*, 324. exp. 4.

[10] Regulations of Father Tomás Altamirano, Aug. 28, 1679. *Archivum Romanum Societatis Jesu* (hereafter cited ARSJ), *Miscellanea Mexicana*, VIII, f. 56v.

[11] *Tanto Simple*, Chapter 9, f. 30ss.

[12] The secularization of twenty-two missions in Sinaloa is a case in point. For several years the Society of Jesus wished to relinquish its missions to the diocese of Durango. Cf. *Autos, testimonios*, and *expedientes* relative to the transfer of the twenty-two missions; *Archivo General de la Nación* (hereafter cited as AGN), *Ramo Jesuitas, Estancia* 1, *Legajo* 16. Regarding the manner and method of the transfer and the payment of alms, see AHH, *Temp.* 540, exp. 2; and AGN, *Historia* 20, exps. 7 and 8. The transfer was less than successful; cf. *Anuas de las misiones de la Provincia de la Nueva España de la Compañía de Jesús, principalmente desde la congregación provincial de noviembre de 1751 hasta la última que se celebró por noviembre de este año 1757*, paragraph 18. This has been published as *Misiones Norteñas Mexicana de la Compañía de Jesús, 1751–1757*, Ernest J. Burrus, editor, p. 22. Father Juan Nentwig noted the difficulty experienced in finding secular volunteers because they feared death at the hands of enemies on the frontier; cf. Juan Nentwig, *Rudo Ensayo*, p. 147.

the *reducción*.[13] Unfortunately, reducción has taken on misleading conno-
tations in the English literature of mission history. Its literal translation as
"reduction" seems to imply a form of slavery, which is an inadmissible
inference both from the intent of the law on reducciones as well as from the
record of history.[14] Second, the term has become closely identified with
the Jesuit missions of Paraguay. These missions were reducciones within
the intent and scope of the Laws of the Indies, but these same laws applied
equally to the historical phenomenon of missions in other Spanish possessions.

Generically the term applies to an incipient community where the Indians
have been gathered together for more efficient and effective administration,
both spiritual and temporal. The intention behind forming reducciones was
to "lead the Indian back" from the mountains and woods into a community
where he could better learn the rudiments of Christian belief and the
elementary forms of Spanish social and political organization.[15] Under
the law the Jesuit missions of New Spain were reducciones in the same
sense as the Jesuit missions of Paraguay. This does not imply, however, that
the two missionary efforts were not distinct. The Paraguay reducciones were
large, civilized complexes that outweighed the smaller, scattered Spanish
communities.[16] By contrast the missions of northwestern New Spain were
liberally interspersed with *reales de minas* and colonial pueblos.

The terms conversión, doctrina, and reducción express qualitative aspects
of a mission. When a mission is considered administratively, a different set
of terms is employed. Often a document merely uses the term "misión"
without specific reference to the particular administrative unit connoted; here
again, the context determines the meaning. The broadest administrative unit
to which the term misión applied was the mission province, such as the
"mission of the Tarahumara" or the "mission of Sonora." As in the case of
early Sinaloa and Sonora, the mission province was co-extensive with the
political province. Although the provincial divisions of the missions normally
followed the civil pattern, they did not always coincide, particularly in
the later years of Jesuit missionary activity when some longer established
missions were secularized, thus leaving other missions administratively
dependent on mission provinces outside the civil province.[17]

A mission province was an aggregate of large administrative units
called *rectorados*, which, in turn, consisted of several *cabeceras* and their
visitas. The administrative head of the mission province was legally the
Jesuit Provincial in Mexico City, but in practice each province was handled
by a Father Visitor, delegated by the Provincial. After 1723 several mission

---

[13] *Titulo 3, Libro VI.*
[14] Cf. Hubert Clinton Herring, *History of Latin America from Beginnings to the Present*, p. 180 sq., or Bailey Wallys Diffie, *Latin American Civilization: Colonial Period*, p. 198 sq. "Utilizing" Indians is an unfair characterization. The Indians were in fact employed and permitted over half their time to work their own lands.
[15] *Recopilación, Ley 1, Titulo 3, Libro VI.*
[16] Excellent information on the Jesuit reducciones of Paraguay can be found in Guillermo Fúrlong Cardiff, *Misiones y sus pueblos de guaraníes;* also, a series of documentary articles by Francisco Mateos in *Ebenda,* 1947 through 1953.
[17] In the mid-eighteenth century transfers and closures created this situation in Sinaloa, Nayarit, Topía, and parts of the Tarahumara.

provinces were overseen by a Visitor General with the powers of a Vice-provincial; each mission province still maintained a Father Visitor who had immediate care of his one province.[18]

The mission rectorado comprised several *partidos* or districts. In administrative control was a Rector, or immediate religious superior. In the Jesuit system, the Rector was responsible for the normal conduct of all missionaries within the rectorado; his availability to the Fathers on the mission was understood to be constant and immediate. He was expected to watch over internal discipline and resolve the more immediate problems that might arise. He could grant ordinary permissions and dispense subjects from minor obligations. The usual term of office for a Rector was three years, as with most canonical appointments.[19] The appointment of Rectors was reserved to the Provincial of New Spain who customarily followed the recommendations of the Father Visitor in charge of the particular mission province.[20]

The rectorado was divided into several partidos, or perhaps more accurately, the rectorado was built up from several partidos because the establishment did not precede the division. A mission province grew from little more than a mission center and a few visitas. As missions multiplied in number, eventually they would constitute a new rectorado; then, two or three rectorados would be joined into a new mission province.[21] In other words, an administrative system was not predesigned and imposed on a territory. Furthermore, because the established missions were slow in achieving full acculturation, the administrative system had to grow more complex to provide for the diversity in the stages of religious and cultural change that were occurring in even one mission sector.

The *partido* derives its definition from the rectorado. It is a division of the rectorado and occasionally is called a *distrito*. There was no minimum or maximum area set down for a partido; rather, a partido consisted of a cabecera and visitas, or a head mission and mission stations. The partido was assigned to one or two Fathers depending on the availability of missionaries and the extent of the territory. Although the rule originally called for the missionaries to work in pairs, the vast expanse of mission territory soon dictated that a single man had to provide for two, three, and even four or more churches.[22] Thus the partido became the basic building block of the mission system.

A missionary assigned to a designated partido ministered to several Indian pueblos and rancherías. Ordinarily he resided at the largest Indian village where he supervised the construction of a large, ample church. In the smaller and outlying villages or rancherías smaller churches were con-

---

[18] AHH, *Temp.* 1126, exp. 3; also ARSJ, *Misc. Mex.* 9, f. 387.

[19] Cf. the *Code of Canon Law*, canon 505. The current codification was not in effect during the missionary epic, but the Council of Trent had insisted in following this long-standing practice in the Church.

[20] Cf. Instruction of Father Arjó to Father Guendulain, ARSJ, *Misc. Mex.* 9, f. 387. See Part Two of this text, pp. 105-114.

[21] For an illustration of this procedure see Eusebio Francisco Kino, *Kino's Memoirs of the Pimería Alta*, Herbert E. Bolton translator, Book II, p. 97.

[22] Cf. *Rules of Father Visitor Rodrigo de Cabredo*, Rule 1; Part Two of this text, p. 61.

structed that acted as visitas. The mission of residence was known as the cabecera, which is quite adequately translated as "headquarters." Beyond the fact that the missionary spent·more time and effort on the cabecera, although this, too, was controlled, the cabecera enjoyed no other particular distinction.[23]

In the earliest stages of evangelization a missionary decided on an Indian village as his mission of residence. Other Indians of the same tribe would be invited to live at this village; sometimes they were forcibly brought to the chosen village so they could be systematically exposed to the processes of cultural change.[24] Once a village was designated as a cabecera there was still no guarantee that the headquarters mission for that partido would always remain there. Shifts in Indian population or residence would often enough demand that the cabecera be changed. Moreover, missionaries who opened up new regions frequently selected their visitas as sites for future cabeceras in an orderly program of expansion and intensification.[25] Quite simply, cabeceras held their designation because of the missionary in residence. Individual missions frequently changed their status from cabecera to visita, or vice-versa, in the rise and fall of fortunes on the frontier.

The *visita* is most commonly a mission station at a smaller Indian village or ranchería. But the term itself, in mission literature, also has broader applications, as when a whole mission province is described as a "visita" in relation to the Father Visitor. Since the literal meaning is merely "visited," it is no surprise that the term is used relative to the administrator visiting. For example, a mission *station* is a visita with respect to the resident missionary; a *series of partidos* are visitas with respect to the mission's Rector; a *group of rectorados* are visitas with respect to the Father Visitor. The most common use of the term, however, is in regard to the small mission station.

The normal visita had at least a temporary church, a ramada, and/or a priest's house with a few improvements that might assist the missionary in his work. In the circumstances of life on the frontier many full scale cabeceras receded to the status of visitas because resident priests were lacking, the Indian population declined, or rebellion and warfare prevented the continuance of missionary activity. Conversely, however, many visitas had fine churches and residences which were built for eventual transfer to a resident missionary or a secular clergyman when the village achieved full growth.

The preceding terms are the most common ones seen in mission documents. In different epochs and specific documents there are nuances of

---

[23] Cf. remarks of Father Arjó to Guendulain, Part Two, p. 109; and the ruling of an anonymous Father Visitor, p. 120.

[24] For an example of forceful relocation see the letter and reply of Father Vincente del Aguilar to the Visitor, Father Leonardo Xarino (Jatino), Ures, Aug. 7, 1640; AHH, *Temp.* 278, exp. 55.

[25] This was the established method used in the river missions of Sinaloa during the time of Father Andrés Pérez de Ribas. Kino outlines a similar approach in his life of Father Saeta where he briefly describes new visitas and their potential; Eusebio Francisco Kino, *Vida de Francisco Xavier Saeta,* published as *Kino's Biography of Francisco Javier Saeta,* Book Six, pp. 152-181.

meaning as well as inaccuracies in usage. Most of these variant uses can be explained by presuppositions about mission organization. In the earliest period, from 1590 through 1670, the terminology was less precise because the system had not yet grown so complex. "Partido" is a good example. Superficially a partido was synonymous with a distrito. Closer analysis, however, indicates that a partido frequently had less definite boundaries than the distrito. Both were divisions of a rectorado, but the partido had the potential of further division or restriction. Placing these terms in a developmental model, the sequence would begin with the erection of a misión; then, a rectorado would be designated with its combination of partidos, and finally the rectorado would stabilize into distritos. No such formal sequence has been noted in administrative documents, but the conclusion is justified from general observation of the sources.[26]

Ecclesiastical administration closely paralleled the mission system, which was itself subject, in certain ways, to hierarchical organization and practice. At the highest level the Jesuit Province of New Spain resembled a diocese, but its territorial jurisdiction far outreached any of the dioceses of Mexico. The frontier mission province compares with a vicariate, but vicariate structures were weak or non-existent throughout the northern frontier. In the case of northwestern New Spain the Bishops of Guadalajara and Guadiana (Durango) continually disputed the extent of their jurisdiction over the missions.[27] Although administratively independent of the episcopacy, the missionaries were cautioned to maintain harmony between the order and the hierarchy.

The tensions that arose between the Orders and the hierarchy were caused, in part, by the fundamental relationships between Church and State in the Spanish empire, as manifested through the Patronato Real. As churches, the missions fell within the sphere of the Bishops' power and influence. As missions, it was the King who designed and supported the missionary program, and it was the King who held appointive power over the Bishops.[28] And if this were not complicated enough, the Holy See granted the exemptions and privileges under which the religious orders operated. Through the Patronato Real the King also exerted power over the papally sanctioned privileges.

Because a missionary had the local care of an Indian community, it is tempting to speak analogously of the missionary's "parish." But the traditional, feudal parish, with its determinate boundaries and closely regulated care of the faithful by a pastor, is not the proper analog for a mission. The concept of an Indian community as neophytes and wholly dependent "chil-

---

[26] See Juan de Almonacir, *Catálogo de los Rectorados y Misiones de las Provincias de Sinaloa y Sonora*, Feb. 17, 1685; AHH, *Temp.* 1126, exp. 4. Almonacir recorded even long established missions as "located on the frontier."

[27] Cf. *Disertación acerca de la potestad de los obispos de la Nueva Vizcaya sobre los misioneros y misiones de la Compañía de Jesús*, AHH, *Temp.* 2009, exp. 23.; also the decisions of the Royal Courts over California jurisdiction, AGI, *Guad.* 67-3-28/9 (Pastell's Vol. 27, p. 279).

[28] Cf. William Eugene Shiels, *King and Church: The Rise and Fall of the Patronato Real.*

dren" distinguishes the mission from a parish which was conceived, rightly or wrongly, as a community of mature faithful who depended on the church for little else than requisite spiritual ministry. Because the feudal parish was designed around the vassalage of a self-sustaining community, it was legally vulnerable to many kinds of taxation and tithing. Consequently the missionaries were almost overly cautious never to call their missions parishes.[29]

Parishes or *curatos* are frequently encountered in the Spanish *reales de minas* along the frontier. Documentary usage seems to favor curato over *parroquia;* parroquia implies a more permanent establishment. The Jesuit missionaries were under precept never to sign their names as "curas" because such a formality would indicate an allegiance to episcopal authority that would conflict with religious obedience.[30]

The mission territory of northern New Spain was not the exclusive domain of the Society of Jesus. Eastward along the Sierra Madre Occidental the Franciscan friars labored in an equally vast region. Although both religious orders engaged in missionary evangelization, the particular form of religious life within the two orders gave rise to a different set of administrative regulations. One of the problems that has developed in the study of mission history is the tendency to view missionary labors univocally. The orders shared the same primary and secondary goals: the salvation of souls and the conversion of indigenous peoples. But the methods the various orders employed were conditioned by the *Leyes de Indias,* royal cédulas, and the institutes of the religious orders themselves. These influences did not evoke uniform responses.

Indeed, the evolution of the mission systems of the two orders followed distinctly different paths. The early Jesuit efforts were somewhat individualistic as the regulations disclose. The Franciscan approach in the early seventeenth century stemmed from a group or team; in the last quarter this developed into the system of apostolic colleges which was wholly distinct from the Jesuit manner of recruitment, training, and support. The earliest Franciscan entry into Sonora was attempted along the traditional lines of establishing a *custodia.* The Franciscan custodia as an administrative unit falls midway between the Jesuit mission province and rectorado. The administrative powers of a Franciscan *custodio* were less extensive than those of a Jesuit Visitor, but more extensive than those of a Jesuit Rector.

Normally the Franciscan custodia comprised several conventos, or residences for the friars. A convento was roughly equivalent to a cabecera because it was the headquarters for the missionary friars. In the Franciscan approach a mission residence was presumed to fulfill the requirements for a convent or community, although this was frequently not the case. In the Jesuit system there was no intention that a missionary should live in a community. It was sufficient that he had occasional contact with fellow religious in the territory. So, while it might appear that the two orders followed the

---

[29] Documentary sources seldom confuse these terms; the analogy is more commonly found in lay literature about the missions.

[30] Cf. Regulations of Father Tomás Altamirano, Number 4; Part Two of this text, p. 85.

same pragmatic course of assigning one missionary to one church, the two
orders actually experienced very different internal tensions in maintaining
their religious identity and in resolving the problems of methodology in their
ministry.[31] Both orders, however, were careful to designate their mission
residences as religious houses and their work as that of clerics regular, thus
maintaining their distinction from all aspects of the secular clergy. Whole
sets of rules and canonical regulations applied to the religious as well as
their residences, so the distinction asserted here goes beyond an exercise in
semantics; these rules affected daily living and the ministry.[32] Jesuits and
Franciscans shared the apostolic goals of the Roman Catholic Church, but
each order was characterized by a deeply different asceticism. Some may
legitimately study the grand sweep of missionary organization, but the minuscule rules of daily life and the ascetical goals of the missionaries themselves
shaped their effectiveness with the native peoples.

---

[31] Methodology will be discussed in detail in the chapter on mission methodology.

[32] Not only was the Jesuit missionary subject to specific mission regulations, but he
carefully observed the Rules of the Society, the Common Rules, the Rules of Modesty, the
Rules for Preachers and Confessors, the Rules for Superiors, and the spirit of the Institute.
These rules applied to what clothes had to be worn, how often rooms had to be swept, how
the head had to be carried, how the eyes had to be cast in speech, how penitents were to
be counselled, and so forth. Little was left to individual freedom. Life on the missions was
not a flight from their observance; on the contrary, men were selected for the missions on
their ability to maintain perfect observance while living outside a cloister or religious
community.

The Jesuit Mission System: Rules and Precepts

he rules and precepts by which the Jesuit mission system operated provide the best evidence of its evolution from simple evangelization to a complex social institution. The investigation of these rules and precepts casts considerable light on the complexities of an apostolic endeavor that many are tempted to oversimplify merely because the mission was a frontier institution. These rules constitute the norms by which the missions should have operated, but no claim can be made that each mission or missionary complied with unfailing exactitude. Yet the changes and amplifications in the rules and precepts attest to changing situations the mission apostolate experienced.

An historical analysis of constitutions, rules or by-laws invites the fallacy of concluding how history should have been instead of how, in fact, it was. The rules and precepts governing the mission system are no exception; only an historical commentary can establish their worth. Fortunately, however, the historian can place proportionately more weight on the rules and precepts of the Jesuit mission system as indicators of historical reality than he might on a civil constitution. The reason for this rests in the asceticism peculiar to the Society of Jesus — the Ignatian stress on obedience. It was the intention of Ignatius Loyola, the founder, that his men would distinguish themselves in the service of the Church by their unquestionable obedience to the Holy Father and to the least rule of the Institute by which the sons of Ignatius were recognized as a religious order.[1]

While the emphasis insisted upon by Ignatius shaped the character of the post-Reformation order, it also set up scrupulous tensions among the Jesuits who found themselves facing limitless problems that strained their dedication and imagination. The rules and precepts by which the missions

---

[1] The Society of Jesus was established through the Papal Bull of Paul III, *Regimini militantis ecclesiae*, Sept. 27, 1540. Paragraphs three to eight are commonly called the "Formula of the Institute." Pope Julius III confirmed the Formula on July 21, 1550, in his Bull, *Exposcit debitum*. The particular stress on obedience is in paragraph 4.

Ignatius penned a famous "Letter on Obedience" to the scholastic community at Coimbra, Portugal, Mar. 26, 1533. That letter became an ascetical classic in Jesuit formation and was read monthly in all Jesuit houses of formation. He states: "Of course, I wish you to be perfect in all spiritual gifts and adornments. But it is especially in the virtue of obedience, as you have heard from me on other occasions, that I am anxious to see you signalize yourselves." (Paragraph 2).

of northwestern New Spain were governed show the minuscule concern of superiors for exact observance. Because the perfection of the religious life depended largely on such exact observance of the rule in the minds of the Jesuit missionaries, it is a most reasonable assumption that these rules were truly the norms of conduct. What the rules demanded was most probably what the men actually did. Some rules and precepts were violated through necessity, but such infractions were constantly under discussion and violators frequently punished. These cases provide a fairly accurate gauge in measuring the difficulties that confronted the missionaries.

The collection of rules and precepts on which this study is based belonged at one time to the mission rectorado of San Francisco Borja in Sonora.[2] The major portion of the rules pertained to all the missions as well as to the rectorados of Sonora. Specific rules were issued by the Fathers Provincial or Visitor; these enjoyed the force of a "precept." The precepts enjoined the subjects who fell within its provisions under the stricture of serious sin against the vow of obedience. Although such religious rulings were not backed up by civil law as such, the widespread power of ecclesiastical courts, and the ever present threat of inquisitorial authority, usually brought strict and early compliance by the subject in the event he found the ruling difficult to obey for ascetical reasons.[3]

The first code of rules for the government of the missions was issued under the authority of Father Rodrigo de Cabredo in 1610. Cabredo is a relatively unknown figure in early Mexican Jesuit history, but he was responsible for setting the tempo of apostolic activity in New Spain for almost two decades. His first assignment in the New World was to the Province of Peru where he acted as Provincial from 1598 to 1604. He came to New Spain as Visitor General when the province's hierarchical structure seems to have been in flux; the province was being governed at the time (1609) by Father Martín Peláez, who only held the office of Vice-provincial. Following a term of visitation for over a year, Cabredo was appointed Provincial of New Spain in 1611 and served until 1616.[4]

The Code of 1610 was approved by Father Cabredo and bears his name, but the Code itself was the product of an assembly of representatives from all the missions. A junta had been convened at Durango in 1609, just after the arrival of Cabredo. Peláez, writing to Father General Claudius Acquaviva in Rome, informed him that the junta had been held in Durango so that mission affairs could be straightened out and a superior appointed over all of

---

[2] The rules, regulations, precepts and letters for this study were taken from material gathered and deposited in the Roman Archives of the Society of Jesus. Scholars have referred to this collection under the designation of ARSJ, *Miscellanea Mexicana, Tomo IX*. Research at the Archivo Histórico de Hacienda in Mexico City has revealed that many of the original documents are located in AHH, *Temp*. 1126. From internal evidence it seems clear that the ARSJ collection was taken from the AHH documents, but the Jesuit collection benefits from being more complete. The initial compilation and identification of the rules was made by Gerard Decorme, S.J.; the paleography was done by Felix Zubillaga, S.J.

[3] The matter is unduly complicated; cf. Farriss, *Crown and Clergy*.

[4] Cf. ARSJ, *Mex*. 2, ff. 90-142 and 142v-331.

them. This was done to conform to orders which had been received from Rome.[5]

This junta marks the first organized stage in the development of the missions of the northwest. Up to this time, the missionaries were appointed by the Provincial and answerable either to him or to the Rector of a college. Prior to this, the various missions were not without a superior, but there was no superior for all the missions.[6] The assignment of missionaries still rested with the Provincial, but the expansion of the apostolate in the last decade of the sixteenth century strained the administrative apparatus of Jesuit New Spain.

Cabredo's rules sounded the customary note of religious companionship in that "Ours," that is, Jesuits, should accompany one another two by two; the rule was tinged with Ignatian asceticism because one of the companions was to be subject to the other. The obedience-minded Jesuits were feeling the burden of isolated missionary existence. In actuality the companionship rule, which many ascetical writers felt was a safeguard of the religious vows, was seldom followed.

The latter part of the rule counselled a frequent interchange among neighboring missionaries, which became a true hallmark of Jesuit missionary existence.[7] Communication between missionaries of different districts was intended for the spiritual and human well-being of the men who had to live apart from the more familiar settings of Spanish daily life.[8] And communication with the appointed superiors was insisted on because independence of action was greatly feared — on ascetical, not prudential, grounds. The vastness of the mission frontier and the natural demands of self-reliance posed a threat to the obediential asceticism of the Society.

The missionaries were expected to consult with the superior before every important move, and even in the event of a superior's absence, a full report was to be made afterwards. To the casual observer it might appear that the freedom of movement among the missionaries was restricted only by the fear of the unknown and the limitations of an individual's stamina, but the men assigned to the frontier missions were not even permitted to make *entradas* among pagan tribes without prior approval, usually written, from a

---

[5] Peláez held the position of Vice-provincial because the General had not yet appointed a provincial; Cabredo held the superior powers of a Visitor General. Cf. ARSJ, *Mex.* 2 f. 133.

The letter is cited in Alegre, ABZ, II, p. 199, without date. The letter from Acquaviva ordering the junta and the appointment of a superior is recorded in ARSJ, *Mex.* 2, f. 110. All the *"Padres graves"* were summoned from the missions to participate in the junta at Durango. Apparently Father Hernando de Villafañe was named "superintendent" of the missions "adentro," ARSJ, *Mex.* 2, f. 143.

[6] For the early operation of the mission system, see Andrés Pérez de Ribas, *Corónica y historia.*

[7] Frequent communication among missionaries is common knowledge. For an example of the frequency, see the correspondence of Kino with Father Francisco Xavier Saeta in Polzer-Burrus, *Kino's Biography of F. J. Saeta.*

[8] Early missionaries dwelled on the theme of isolation and privation. See the comments of Father Laurencio Adame in a letter to Cabredo, Sinaloa, Jan. 16, 1610; he expressed joy at ministering to such a needy tribe, whose needs he himself shared. Also the Viceroy's nephew, Father Luis de Velasco, stressed the completely different way of life on the Sinaloa frontier. ABZ, II, pp. 199-200.

major superior. In Cabredo's code the obvious concern was to prevent over-extension whether in manpower or money. This concern persisted in later restrictions by various provincials, but the reasons underlying it shifted grounds.[9]

One of the lesser known but probably the most stressed rule was that of the semi-annual *junta*.[10] These juntas were really an application of the Rules of the Society of Jesus that its members were to renew their religious vows each six months. The vows could have been renewed without a group meeting, so the purpose of the juntas was more than renewal alone. The Cabredo Code stressed that the men attending the junta should maintain a daily schedule similar to that observed in the colleges. There was latent fear that the independence of living on the frontier would erode the routine of religious life, not to mention the envy (euphemistically termed "scandal") that missionary freedom created in the stricter college communities. Despite the importance placed on the junta, the rule was difficult to observe because of obligations on the missions. Eventually the juntas were limited to no more than three Fathers and were never convened during major feasts.

While the junta functioned for the Society as an occasion of religious renewal, the gatherings also provided opportunities for the missionaries to discuss methods and share observations they had made about Indians in their charge. Unfortunately, no minutes or records of these juntas have come to light; the topics of discussion were of things "that cannot be found in the books" or in the disputations of learned doctors.[11] In effect the juntas bound the missionaries into a closely cooperative unit. Although the normal isolation and apostolic burdens weighed heavily on each man, the juntas rekindled zeal and dedication for the difficult lives the men were leading.[12] Because of the shortage of manpower and the subsequent inability of some men to attend the two juntas, superiors later insisted that everyone attend at least one meeting annually. Failure to comply with this directive meant the immediate superior of the mission had to notify the Provincial.[13]

The juntas also became the occasions at which the missionaries filed their annual *memorias* or requests for supplies to be purchased from their alms. Brief note sheets were sent on to Mexico City to the Province or Mission Procurator; the notes had to be countersigned by either the Rector or the Visitor before being recognized as valid. Generally the mission superiors were present at the juntas, so the procedure of getting a signature was somewhat simplified. The countersigning also provided an opportunity for the superiors

---

[9] Cf. Part 2, p. 64. In the fiftieth rule of Cabredo's revised code these regulations are attributed to Father Alonso de Bonifacio. This should be Father Luis Bonifaz who was Visitor to the Sinaloa missions from 1621 to 1627; cf. Decorme, *La obra*, II, p. 439.

[10] Cf. Part 2, p. 64, rule 14.

[11] Cf. *Relación delo sucedido en el plieto de la Comp* con los Religiosos del S*n* Fran*co*, anonymous manuscript, circa 1665; AHH, *Temp.* 1126, *exp.* 2, f. 2sq. In recounting the struggle between the Franciscans and Jesuits over jurisdiction in the Valley of Sonora, the document portrays how the juntas were employed. See also, Part Two, p. 64, regarding the impracticality of the doctors.

[12] The rule enjoined the superior to give an exhortation or conference which would stimulate the missionaries' zeal. Part Two, p. 64, rule 14.

[13] Part Two, p. 65, rule 15.

to review and compare the itemized lists while the missionaries were still assembled. An individual missionary might request more than an average amount of certain items, such as chocolate or clothing; the superiors could then correct any excess or appeal to other missionaries to contribute to the needs of their brother. Although the missions were manifestly in need throughout most of their history, the Society always expressed great concern that the missionaries observe a strict personal poverty. The juntas helped both the superiors and the subjects focus on the spirit of the religious vows, especially in such mundane matters as the annual memorias. Engulfed in immediate needs, an isolated priest might be tempted to ask for more than religious poverty would allow.

The sixteen paragraphs of Cabredo's Code were a simple compendium of directives that stressed the concern the missionaries held for the Indians. Although isolation dominated some of the rules, the overall tone demonstrated a conscious gentleness and desire to maintain cooperative measures with the Indians and the Spaniards for the greater good of all. The Jesuits were cautioned to minister to the Spanish communities whenever occasion required, but this was never to be done at the expense of the primary ministry to Indians. For example, Indian labor was not a free market open to the Spaniards. The Fathers were encouraged to counsel the Spanish *repartidores* (or labor distributors), but they were not permitted to parcel out Indian labor for neighboring haciendas. At the same time, the missionaries were directed to train their Indian charges in productive works along the theme that a "busy Indian is a peaceful one."[14]

Cabredo's Code also enjoined the learning of the native languages, a practice that all superiors continually stressed. The code required the missionary to reduce any new language to rules; the missionary was directed to seek assistance by Indians who knew both the native language and Spanish. A newcomer was expected to learn the language from other priests who had already mastered it. But the practice of the rule was not easy. Sometimes priests who had learned the language were transferred or died without having had a chance to train younger men. As a result, the learning of the difficult dialects of the northwest always posed a serious problem for the missionaries.

For fifty-two years Cabredo's Code remained in effect; these fundamental guidelines were only modified by occasional, specific precepts from Provincials or Visitors. Then, in 1662, Father Visitor Hernando de Cabrero convened a new assembly of missionaries at the Jesuit College of Guadalajara. The missionaries had been complaining that the existing code was filled with too many unattainable rules. Moreover, the circumstances had changed so noticeably on the frontier, many rules were no longer applicable.[15]

Cabrero himself had only recently arrived in Mexico; he had come to the Province with the powers of Visitor in 1661. Like Cabredo he plunged immediately into the problems presented by the missions. He listened to the

---

14 Part Two, p. 64, rule 12.
15 Part Two, p. 61, Introduction.

missionaries' viewpoints on three separate occasions in order to determine a suitable course of action. The first meeting was at Guadalajara in March, 1662; the second was held at the novitiate of Santa Ana in Mexico City a month later. With a summer intervening to review the findings, Cabrero, Father Provincial Pedro Antonio Díaz, and the Province consultors finally settled on a new code September 20, 1662. These rules became, in effect, the governing laws for the next century of Jesuit missionary labors in New Spain. The only major modification to these rules came in 1723 with the establishment of a Visitor General for the missions, but this was purely administrative, not formulative.[16]

The missionaries and Cabrero held differing sentiments about the goals and the apostolate of the missions. Cabrero felt a missionary's work was primarily conversion. He believed the Jesuits of New Spain were too deeply engaged in work as doctrineros, that is, in instructing the already-converted Indians. At the sixteenth Provincial Congregation, held in Mexico City in November, 1662, Cabrero expressed his inclination to abandon the missions and entrust them to the secular clergy. His approach was to resume the missionary method being employed in central Mexico which depended on a college staff that periodically visited neighboring Indian pueblos to give brief courses in Christian doctrine. Cabrero advocated leaving the missions of Sinaloa where the Indians were fewer in number.[17]

The opinions of Visitor Cabrero did not prevail. The delegates to the provincial congregation strongly opposed his propositions and the General of the Society ultimately acquiesced to the views of the Province.[18] The reasons lodged against Cabrero's proposals were: 1) the old methods had proven successful; 2) the college-based system was not practical for missions over 400 leagues distant from Mexico; 3) no college could supply the sixty or more missionaries that were required; 4) without special permission of the Viceroys no missionary could enter new regions to convert the Indians — at least not without grave danger to their lives; 5) there were no seculars to take over the care of the converts; 6) it would be more appropriate, apostolically, to care for Indian neophytes than to expose them to apostasy; 7) if the Jesuits were to leave the missions, 45,129 souls would be lost that were actually in the Society's care — not to mention the loss in alms![19]

The difference of viewpoints between Cabrero and the Province consultors had obvious importance. The Visitor was arguing for a change of method while issuing orders at the same time for a more minute control of the existing system. The fifty-one paragraphs of Cabrero's code are far more exacting than the outmoded rules of Cabredo. At Guadalajara the missionaries confided that many of the original rules were no longer pertinent, but those simple and direct provisions could hardly have worked difficulties comparable to the lengthy strictures of the 1662 code. Perhaps the discrep-

---

[16] Part Two, p. 66, Regulations for the Visitors.
[17] ARSJ, *Congregaciones* 76, f. 151v. sq.
[18] Ibid., f. 149.
[19] The loss in alms refers to the loss in income from the Royal Treasury which was paid annually to each mission.

ancy is attributable to Cabrero's inexperience. Certainly the subsequent precepts of Provincials and Visitors indicated that the 1662 revision failed to solve the problems experienced under the 1610 code. The missionaries only had more rules to follow after 1662, and many of them were even less attainable than some in the 1610 code.

Cabrero regulated the number of mules in packtrains, and even the number of books a man might take in transferring from one mission to another. In fairness to Cabrero, whose name the 1662 code bears, it should be remembered that the rules were probably formulated by delegates to the various congregations prior to the final formulation. Cabrero could scarcely have known how many mules it would take to return from a frontier he had never seen. The 1662 Code is filled with references to proper relations between the Jesuits and the Spaniards on the mission frontier. This contrasts sharply with the earlier code in that the missionaries formerly were only cautioned to assist the neighboring Spaniards whenever possible and as long as such assistance did not deter the Fathers from their primary responsibilities to the Indians. The Cabrero Code regulates contact with the Spaniards, commerce with them, communication, and even proscribes the Fathers from soliciting material goods for their welfare. There is almost a preponderance of concern for the material workings of the established missions, which would lend a great deal of support to Cabrero's contention that the missions were already beyond the point where Jesuits should have ceased to be of service.

Herein lies the problem of the evolution of the Jesuit mission system; the missions had become something other than what they were originally conceived to have been. The point in dispute was whether Christian baptism converted the Indian to Spanish society, or whether the purposes of missionary conversion also extended to the processes of acculturation. The judgment of the men of the time was that a missionary's work did not stop with the acceptance of the waters of baptism. The missions would have had to build buffers around the neo-Christian communities until those who had accepted new religious beliefs could compete and survive in a culture that was possibly more hostile than peaceably Christian. Cabrero's Code leaves no doubt that the Jesuit missionaries were expected to walk the narrow path between inspiring the Indians and not scandalizing the Spaniard.

Even a cursory reading of the 1662 Code reveals a latent reaction to situations that must have commonly occurred on the frontier. The number of days the Indians could work, the hours they had to attend Mass and the doctrina, the number of lashes permitted in flogging, the exactness with which mission records were to be filled, the days of feasting and the number of dishes served — all were stipulated, and the major superiors expected them to be obeyed. In a half century the life of a missionary had become understandably complex. No new mission, regardless of its distance from Mexico City, would be free from the burden of conscience the missionary had to bear because he knew his religious perfection depended on the precision of his obedience. He was caught between protecting the Indian from exploitation and instructing him rapidly enough to assume a responsible role in Spanish society. Through the years the Jesuit mission system concentrated less on expanding the frontiers of conversion than in educating the Indians already converted. Cabrero's criticism of the mission became, in effect, the heart of the mission system.[20]

As in the case of the 1610 Code, an advance in the administrative structure of the mission system was made with the promulgation of the new rules. At that time the Durango junta called for the appointment of a superior for all the missions because the resident missionaries were too occupied with the continual visitation of Indian pueblos. This superior had to visit the entire mission field, taking account of the spiritual and temporal welfare of each Father and each mission. In turn, the superior had to notify the Provincial of the situations that existed throughout the various mission districts.

By the mid-seventeenth century the number and dispersion of the missions was so great that no one superior could handle the job. The mission partidos were grouped into rectorados, the rectorados were arranged in provinces, and the provinces were placed in charge of a Father Visitor. Although the office of Visitor had been instituted long before 1662, doubts had arisen about the extent of his jurisdiction. Much of the actual control of mission affairs was left to the Rectors because the different native tribes and the varying socio-economic conditions called for distinct solutions. On the other hand, the growing complexity of ecclesiastical, civil, and military relations necessitated the office of a Visitor who could transcend the particulars of a given problem and coordinate appeals and requests made at the higher levels of government.

Consequently, Father Provincial Pedro Antonio Díaz and the consultors issued a short compendium of rules for the Fathers Visitor in September, 1662, together with the general code for all the missions. To clarify the nature of the Visitor's jurisdiction the compendium stipulated that the primary purpose for instituting the office was to supply for the inability of the Provincial to make a yearly visitation of his subjects on the mission frontiers.[21] A complaint had been registered that Visitors, unlike Provincials, did not relinquish the exercise of authority after the completion of a visitation. Because the Rectors of houses, colleges, or missions were autonomous in most matters, the Visitor was only expected to intervene in extraordinary or reserved cases. Díaz's solution was to surround each Visitor with a board of consultors, appointed by the Provincial; the consultors themselves served on the same mission as the Visitor. Thus the Visitor's power was checked by making him responsible to men not of his choosing.

Díaz insisted that the reason for the institution of the office was to make possible a semi-annual inspection of the missions. Following each visitation, the Visitor had to file a report to the Provincial, who then made the ordinary decisions. In urgent cases the Visitor did have the power to discipline a religious by expelling him from the missions to one of the colleges at Guadalajara or Durango. Missionaries, when they considered an entrada among

---

[20] This discussion has involved the Code of Father Hernando Cabrero, 1662; cf. Part Two, pp. 66-75.

[21] The Society maintained a strict policy on the account of conscience; cf. *Rules for Provincials*, Rule 48, *Regulae Societatis Jesu* (Rome: Curia Praepositi Generalis, 1947).

pagan tribes was in order, had to bring the request to the Visitor; only the Visitor had the authority to deal with the various Captains and Governors who could sanction such ventures. In resolving disputes the Visitor was only permitted to change men from their districts with grave cause and after consultation. Appointment to missions remained a prerogative of the Provincial. Indeed, the Visitor was a powerful figure, but he was an administrator and not an executive. Not until the first quarter of the eighteenth century was a post created, that of the Visitor General, that held truly executive powers.[22]

The collection of rules and precepts that belonged to the rectorado of San Francisco Borja in Sonora contained several pages of interim rules and precepts made either by Provincials or Visitors. The standing orders were to record these rules in a permanent book at the mission so there would be no possibility of loss or doubt about their authenticity. These same rules were read twice yearly by the priests attending the semi-annual juntas. The 1662 Code required that a copy of the rules and precepts be available for the missionaries' use; in the same spirit the newer modifications were recorded. Several of these modifications cast light on the mission system.

In 1677, fifteen years after the Cabrero Code became operative, Father Provincial Tomás Altamirano ordered a thorough visitation of the missions by Father Juan Ortiz de Zapata, a special Visitor. The northern missions had come under severe criticism and it appeared that an updating of the Cabrero Code was in order.[23]

Ortiz's concerns were properly those of a Visitor; his rules dwelled on the perfection of the religious life among the missionaries. Stressing the exactness and care the Fathers should maintain in their spiritual exercises, he was not ready to accept excuses for failure to celebrate Mass, whether for lack of devotion or lack of wine and hosts. He reiterated the need for the missionaries to attend the juntas at which time they could practice themselves in strict observance "at the sound of the bell."[24]

As for the Indians, the emphasis was on their constant and adequate instruction. A settled pattern of life in the mission pueblo is somewhat more evident because Ortiz wanted regular tolling of the *Angelus* and the *De Profundis* in the cabecera as well as the visitas. Where the missionary was absent, the *fiscales* and catechists were charged with this regular responsibility. Interestingly enough, these rules are the first ones to stipulate care for and repair of the established missions. The actual churches throughout the mission territory were of various ages, but none had yet reached the century mark. Many churches had already fallen down and the expense of rebuilding was no small matter. These same rules also demonstrate a crystalization of the administrative system inasmuch as churches and residences were

---

[22] Part Two, "Rules for Visitors," p. 105.

[23] The criticism stemmed from activities at Mátape. Ortiz de Zapata was a native of Zacatecas and an experienced missionary. Cf. *Relación de las misiones, Documentos para la historia de México*, Series 4, Vol. I, pp. 301-419.

[24] Part Two, "Rules of Father Visitor Juan Ortiz Zapata," p. 81.

not to be changed without consultation or permission. Cabeceras were not easily to be changed.[25]

Accompanying Ortiz de Zapata's rules, Father Provincial Altamirano issued a letter that was to be recorded in the rule book, but the contents of this letter were not to be made known to any non-Jesuit. The reason for Altamirano's order was that the letter dealt with the delicate relationships between the Jesuit missionaries and the northern Bishops. The Society's position was strongly independent. Regarding the building of churches, Altamirano admitted he had sought the Bishop's permission, "but this is by way of courtesy so that he will not feel offended."[26] Although Altamirano obviously accepted the idea of independent Jesuit control of the mission system, he was looking forward to the future relinquishment of the churches. Once the Jesuits left the missions, he opined, the churches will remain behind for the Indians, but the churches will belong to the Bishops. So it would be wise for the Fathers not to load the churches up with finery.[27]

The temporal condition of the missions was a favorite subject of Provincial and Visitors, probably because this was most sensitive to secular criticism and concern. For example, the Cabredo Code (1610) did not touch on the matter of the transferral of missionaries from one district to another, most likely because the system had not yet reached that degree of permanence or stability. The Cabrero Code (1662) ruled that no missionary could take anything from his district that he did not purchase with his alms. Then, in 1681, Father Provincial Bernardo Pardo directed that no missionary could dispose of anything whatsoever from the house or the district, even if it were a chair or a napkin.[28] The Cabrero ruling focused on the justice of the alienation of property; the Pardo regulations concerned the actual material condition of the missions so that, in accord with the General's ruling, "there would be no need for each missionary to set up house anew."[29]

Pardo extended his strictures to require an itemized account of all valuables, including livestock. The formalities of the transfer of a mission had to include the double signatures of the missionary transferring out and the Visitor or the newly appointed missionary. This perhaps accounts for the frequency with which the Visitor accompanied new missionaries to their posts. Because the missions had often been established many years before, the herds were beginning to produce substantial income for the mission districts, so Pardo cautioned the Fathers that only the usufruct of the mission was permitted to be used with permission and within the confines of religious decency.[30]

During the closing quarter of the seventeenth century, the affluence of the missions had become a growing reality. The concern of Visitor and

25 Ibid., pp. 81-83.
26 Part Two. Circular letter, Aug. 28, 1679, p. 84.
27 Ibid., p. 85.
28 Part Two, Circular letter, Sept. 23, 1681, p. 87.
29 Ibid.
30 This freed the missionary from any charge of violating his vow of poverty because he would have had to have title to the property generating the income; the property belonged to the King or Bishop.

Provincials continued to be with material affairs. Father Visitor Juan de Almonacir, however, touched on a few social matters by addressing himself to the problem of prudent punishment of Indian malefactors by forbidding the cutting or binding up of any native's hair, or exceeding eight lashes in event of whipping.[31] Begging had become a prevalent annoyance; Almonacir demanded that the "priests, friars, clerics, and non-clerics . . . who stay for weeks and months" in the mission houses be notified to leave after the third day.[32] Nor were the beggars to be grubstaked for their journey; the Visitor allowed only that they be supplied with bread and food — no silver, mules, or anything else of use or value.[33]

Unfortunately the Sonora missions were for many years the object of malicious slanders and almost ceaseless recriminations. The mining community of San Juan Bautista seems to have sheltered many persons who were discontent with the Jesuit missionaries and the Indians in their charge. Kino repeatedly alluded to the problems the missionaries had with false reports that emanated from this region and the Valley of Sonora.[34] Father Joseph Pallares at Batuc felt impelled to defend the good name of the missions while he was serving in the province.[35] But nothing calmed the storm of claim and counterclaim. Kino's trail companion, Juan Mateo Manje, joined in the battle of words and found himself jailed for maligning the Jesuit Visitor of the Sonora missions.[36]

Whatever specific events or ulterior motives that caused the controversy remain unclear. The polemics, however, attracted the attention of Jesuit superiors who set down strict controls over the associations between missionaries and laymen. Finally, in 1715, after nearly twenty years of disputes, Father Provincial Alonso de Arrivillaga promulgated twenty-one stringent rules to regulate the conduct of the missionaries in order to avoid repetitions of the scandals and charges. Arrivillaga's approach was forceful: if anyone came to discredit the missionaries, the "door was to be shut" in his face. To judge from the content of the rules, the nature of the continuing dispute involved the sale of produce and cattle from the missions.[37] If so, the problem traced back to the stormy relations between Father Daniel Angelo Marras of Mátape and the miners of Sonora.

---

[31] Part Two, Rule 2, p. 89.
[32] Part Two, Rule 4, p. 89.
[33] Part Two, Rules 5 and 6, p. 89.
[34] Kino, *Memoirs*, Vol. I, p. 112sq.
[35] Joseph Pallares, *Defensa Scholastica de las Misiones de Sonora*, AHH, Temp. 17, exp. 70 (1707).
[36] "Arrest and Trial of Juan Mateo Manje," Archivo de Hidalgo del Parral, Chihuahua, Mexico, Año 1707 (hereafter cited as AHP). University of Arizona, Microfilm 318, 1707 A.D., frame 180 sq. General Manje and Captain Pedro Peralta had initiated an *informe* which was given to the Bishop of Durango charging that the Jesuits of Sonora refused to administer the sacraments to Spaniards or to provide Indian labor under the *repartimiento* system. Father Visitor Francisco María Píccolo took exception to the accusations and Manje's wording; this resulted in Manje's summary arrest and imprisonment at Parral for seven months. See also Ernest J. Burrus, *Kino and Manje, Explorers of Sonora and Arizona*. Manje is identified here as the troublesome "lieutenant" at Bacanuche.
[37] Rules SFB, "Regulations for the Missions, Especially Sonora."

The minutiae that caused the scandal undoubtedly made life more difficult for the missionaries. Under the 1715 rules, priests could no longer permit
their foremen to bring their own wives into the mission compounds. And the
Fathers had to make certain that the buttons on their shirts and cassocks
were not made even of imitation gold.[38]

Life had changed on the mission frontier; leisure left time and opportunity enough for scandal. Indeed, mission existence had so stabilized that
the Provincial had to caution the Fathers not to allot temporal goods for
relatives and friends. Arrivillaga was piqued by the consumption of chocolate
which he noted to be the largest single expense for the missions.[39] Affluence
had also come to travel expenses because the missionaries were now restricted
to a 500 peso limit (in silver) to pay their servants in the packtrains that
were not to exceed twenty-four mules. And as with all administrative growth,
rules abounded and ignorance of them compounded; Arrivillaga attacked
the problem with still another rule that all the rules would be read over
every three months, and all ordinary permissions would be renewed every
four months.[40]

Life on the missions was not the virile, spontaneous, free and forthright
existence depicted by romanticists. By the eighteenth century the entire
system had grown so enormously complex that administration itself was a
new problem. More rules and more exact obedience would never cure the
ailments of sheer size. In a little over a century the Jesuit missions along the
river valleys of Sinaloa had sprawled out along the Gulf coast, crept upward
into the mountains, spread into the cactus desert of Sonora and the Pimería
Alta, and had even crossed the Gulf into California. The four mission districts listed in the 1614 catalog had been served by thirty-four Fathers and
four Brothers; in 1720 there were fifteen districts throughout the northwest
served by ninety-one Fathers and one Brother.[41]

The simple promises of support and the modest alms from the Patronato
Real that had sustained Fathers Gonzalo de Tapia and Martín Pérez grew
to a yearly subsidy in 1720 of 38,114 pesos from the Royal treasury and an
accumulated capital debt of 377,086 pesos![42] It is of little wonder, then, that
Father Provincial Joseph de Arjó issued a new compendium of instructions
in 1725 to Father Juan de Guendulain, creating a permanent post of Visitor
General for the missions. The Cabrero Code still served to regulate the
ordinary affairs of the missions, but the appointment of Guendulain constituted the formal recognition of the vast missionary apostolate of the Jesuits
in northwestern Mexico and the need for an on-the-scene authority that
nearly equaled that of the Provincial.[43]

---

[38] Part Two, rule 5, p. 98.

[39] Part Two, p. 100, rule 12. Chocolate was offered to guests according to the custom
on the frontier. Even the General of the Society cautioned the use of chocolate; cf. Oliva
to Andrés Cobián, Mar. 30, 1672, ARSJ, *Mex.* 3, ff. 46v-47.

[40] Ibid., p. 107, rule 13, and p. 108, rule 18.

[41] Cf. ARSJ, *Mex.* 4, f. 203 (1614) and *Mex.* 7, f. 308 sq. (1720).

[42] ARSJ, *Mex.* 6, f. 334v.

[43] Guendulain was appointed Visitor in 1723; the instructions were subsequent. Cf.
Doc. Hist. Méx., Series IV, Vol. IV, p. 22. For instructions see Part Two, pp. 105-114. On
Guendulain, see Donohue, ibid., pp. 43-44.

If nothing else, the appointment of the Visitor General cut decision-making time in half. The Rectors and Visitors of the missions maintained the same powers as before, but instead of having recourse to the Provincial, who was either in Mexico City or on visitation elsewhere in the province, a reply from the Visitor General would suffice. Because the Visitor General was empowered to appoint missionaries, the long delays and extended vacancies that resulted from transfer or death were averted.

Even though the Visitor General's powers were quite extensive, he was held in check by a board of consultors who were named by the Provincial. This method modified the influence of the Visitors of individual missions because they had formerly exercised some of the Provincial's powers by delegation; with the advent of a Visitor General these powers were exercised directly by him. Each Visitor was *ex officio* the Admonitor of the Visitor General whenever the Visitor General was in a Visitor's particular region. All the Visitors together constituted a special board of consultors for matters that touched the common good of the missions. Effectively, this was a better arrangement because, formerly, the individual Visitors were responsible only for their particular region and the Provincial in Mexico City had to coordinate the common welfare of all the missions without benefit of close consultation and immediate knowledge.

Arjó's instructions to the Visitor General were not restricted solely to the creation of the new office; he descended to particulars that amounted to a subtle revision of Cabrero's Code. For example, instead of informing the missionaries about their failures to preach and distribute Communion, he commissioned the Visitor General to make certain these practices were properly executed. Apparently some priests were following the Indian custom of having the sick brought out of their houses to the church for spiritual ministrations; Arjó insisted the sick should remain at home and in bed while the missionaries truly went to visit the sick. Some pueblos still had no churches; he ordered churches to be erected in at least the main pueblos, if not in all the visitas. Furthermore, he laid down new norms for visiting pueblos. Where visitas did exist, the missionaries were directed to celebrate one Sunday Mass each month, and the missionary was expected to remain in the visita two or three days after the Sunday celebration.

Regarding Indian languages, Jesuit policy had not varied. Arjó felt that missionaries could not perform their spiritual duties without having at least a moderate skill in the native dialects. Failure to master a language was cause for removal from a mission; proficiency was cause for a man to remain at the same mission, or at least within the same linguistic region. In some places more than one dialect or language was prevalent. The missionary was expected to know at least one of the more commonly understood languages, although he did not have to know all the languages current in a region. Such a regulation as this indicates that the missions were becoming melting pots for acculturation because the missions in the earlier years of expansion normally ministered to an ethnically and linguistically homogenous group. As the populations of the missions fell in given places, attempts were made to replenish the communities with natives from other linguistic stocks. In the event a mission served different tribes, the minority group in the pueblo frequently spoke the majority language.[44]

Like the Cabrero Code, the instructions to Guendulain frequently refer to relations with laymen. Arjo considered the root of the problem to be too great a familiarity with laymen who exercised too much liberty in talking about affairs internal to the Society. The written word fell under the same strictures as the spoken word, even if the missionaries wrote tracts in "defense" of the missions while at the same time revealing and castigating laymen for their scandalous conduct. The fact that the Provincial included such regulations in his instructions to the Visitor General should signal caution in the use of extant documents. Claims and calumnies abounded on the frontier and these expressions found their way into print and even official documents.[45] Hence, a knowledge of the rules and precepts that governed the missionaries' conduct provides a useful counterbalance to what might appear as factual in the extant records.

Arjó's modifications were not intended to contravene Cabrero's Code; he stressed, rather, the Visitor General's responsibility to oversee careful and adequate surveillance of the missions' temporal welfare. Some missionaries were apt to incur debts for protection of Spanish families; no debts for such reasons were permitted. The permanence of the missions had brought the temptation to utilize them to help others than the Indians for whom they were founded. Arjó graphically denounced the practice by saying that the missions could continue to hire *mayordomos* only "as long as they (the mayordomos) do not suck blood out of the Indians."[46] Exploitation of the weak lurked even in the sanctuary.

The transfer of missionaries was a common practice since the inception of the missions, but Arjó struck a theme not mentioned in previous compendia. When missions that were less arduous became vacant, they were to be assigned to older missionaries, as long as the Fathers were competent in the native language. The extent of the mission system had grown to the point that an internal retirement program had to be instituted. Formerly, the older missionaries were recalled to the colleges where they performed less demanding duties; there the younger men took advantage of their language skills while preparing themselves for future mission assignments. While it is not surprising to see older men reassigned to easier missions, it is worthy to note that these older missions were not relinquished to secular control because there was still need for a ministry in the native languages.[47]

---

44 Arjó, "Compendium of Instructions," Part Two, pp. 105-114. Multiple language skills were commonly required in missions bordering distinct tribal regions. For example, Ures and Cucurpe both had minority groups living at or near the mission. Some early, triennial catalogs list the number of languages each missionary was able to speak. For example, in Sinaloa in 1662 of the sixteen missionaries, nine Fathers spoke two or more Indian languages. In Sonora only one mission, Mobas, required more than one language for proper ministry. Cf. ARSJ, *Mex.* 5, ff. 104-107v.

45 Cf. Luis Navarro García, *Sonora y Sinaloa en el Siglo XVII*. This study is built on large segments of polemical documentation; Navarro García recognized the difficulty of sifting facts from the rhetoric.

46 Part Two, p. 112, rule 45.

47 Ibid., p. 112, rule 51.

The instructions to Father Visitor Guendulain were the last comprehensive code of rules laid down for the missions. Subsequent rules were stated as precepts issued by either the Provincial or the Visitor General. A rule expressed a norm of conduct or procedure that could be dispensed with in case of necessity or with proper permission. A precept was not as easily dispensed from because it bound a subject under pain of sin against his vow of obedience. In a religious order dedicated to spiritual perfection, binding a subject under pain of sin was one of the most stringent and effective methods of gaining compliance. Because a precept was considered a moral command, no room was left for ignorance of the precept; the balance heavily favored scrupulous obedience. The number of precepts was kept low and the subjects were carefully informed. Some precepts had the force of particular law, applying to one mission and not another. So, as the overall system grew in extent and homogeneity, the precepts on the books in different mission provinces occasioned some conflicts and unnecessary restrictions. Provincials and Visitors became concerned about the precepts and began to make resumes of these decretal laws.

Matters governed by precepts were disparate and many. Priests were ordered not to send any silver to the missionaries to support their works; silver could only be sent to the Province Procurator in Mexico City. Spaniards were not to be charged for funeral services. Missions in debt were not to undertake building or furnishing that were in themselves expensive. Card playing was forbidden. New *entradas* among pagan tribes were prohibited. Women cooks were forbidden, and women from the *gente de razón* (educated class) could not serve in the missionary's house. The Fathers were strictly forbidden from having *knowledge* about mining, whether direct or indirect knowledge! And the freedom to contribute alms to worthy causes was successively reduced from fifty pesos to six.[48]

The welter of rule and precept thrust the missionary into sheer confusion about his proper mode of conduct. Some precepts appear as prudent strictures; others, as laws decreed by Provincials in a pique of anger. Father Francisco Xavier Door, the minister of the mission of San Francisco Javier del Batuco in Sonora, compiled a resume of the precepts that had been enjoined on that mission through the years. His listing was relatively simple in comparison to the many precepts which had accumulated in all the missions scattered over the region. Cataloging the precepts which he thought difficult to observe and unsuitable for the purposes for which they were intended, he sent the list on to the Provincial, Father Joseph de Arjo. He carefully explained that he was not attacking the precepts as norms of obedience, but he merely pointed out that these particular decrees were no longer of good service.[49]

Apparently a burst of precept-law was fired at the missions during the provincialate of Father Alejandro Romano (1719–1722). For the most part

[48] Ibid., p. 116, rule 18 and p. 116, rule 20.
[49] Francisco Xavier Door to Joseph de Arjó, Batuco, Sonora, Nov. 29, 1723; AHH, *Temp.* 1126, exp. 1.

Door's objections involved these precepts. Nothing, however, came of his protests because the precepts remained in effect until 1737.

Then, in June, 1737, Father Provincial Juan Antonio de Oviedo dispatched a circular letter revoking many of Romano's precepts.[50] For fifteen years or more the missions had labored under strict rules on the use of money, the sending of gifts to fellow Jesuits in the Province, and the procedures of obtaining permissions. Oviedo relaxed the restrictions on the exchange of items between missionaries and members of the Society as well as relatives. Humanity still breathed among some religious superiors.

An unknown Father left several folio pages of observations concerning the precepts in the book of rules of the mission of San Francisco Borja. Although unsigned and undated, internal evidence points to its being written after the circular letter of Oviedo was issued in 1737. An opinion the anonymous author expressed probably explains the reason for the preservation of the precepts:

> . . . finally, it seems to me that it would be good to make a catalog of the precepts which has to be permanent. It should state that outside of the precepts set down therein, all the rest are hereby suppressed. The Fathers Visitor of the Provinces, during their visitation, should see that each missionary make a copy of it in his presence, and the same Visitors should give them the reasons these are to be observed because otherwise nothing will come from it.[51]

Obviously, the precepts in force in the missions during this period (circa 1740) were a source of confusion to superiors as well as subjects. The same criticism of inconsistency, impracticality, and uselessness was levelled at the rules as at the precepts. The unknown observer believed that each Visitor would have to list all the rules, noting their inconsistencies, and submit them to a board of consultors, who with the Provincial could determine which rules and precepts should or should not apply to particular missions. The efforts at uniformity so cherished by the missionaries of the mid-seventeenth century were falling victim to the much changed circumstances of the mission system in the mid-eighteenth century.[52]

Although the "observations" reveal the delicate manner in which rules and precepts were regarded, the anonymous author was upset by the generalizations by which the precepts were expressed. He attacked the precept

---

[50] Part Two, p. 119. The dating is from AHH, *Temp.* 1126, exp. 1.

[51] ARSJ, *Miscellanea Mexicana, Tomo* IX, f. 400, paragraph 3. Also AHH, *Temp.* 1126, exp. 1.

[52] *Misc. Mex.* IX, f. 477. The manuscript copy of the *observaciones* preserved in the AHH is no longer as complete as the copy in ARSJ. The authorship of the observaciones is difficult to establish, but it would seem that Father Juan Antonio Baltasar, who was Visitor General of the missions in 1744-1747, is the probable author. Much of the correspondence regarding the rules and precepts in the legajos of the AHH are holograph letters from Baltasar who was commissioned to review them. The manuscript copy in the AHH is not in Baltasar's hand, but the style of the language is very similar to his. When Father Provincial Andrés Xavier García issued his "final form" of the precepts, the role of the observations is quite evident. This would suggest that Balthasar was the author because the dates correspond very closely.

against Jesuits playing games, such as checkers or backgammon, in the presence of laymen as being unduly harsh. It so happened in the missions that the Fathers seldom had recreation time to enjoy together, and the scandal that might have resulted from such an innocent game was too inconsequential to justify prohibition.[53] After all, no scandal resulted from laymen "seeing us at play in the gardens," so they should not be offended in seeing Jesuits play a friendly game for pastime.[54]

He criticized the restriction on the number of lashes used to punish Indians. The precept held the number down to eight lashes which the observer felt ought to have been left to the judgment of the Father in the situation, as long as justice and moderation were preserved. "They will only laugh at the Father when they know the eight lashes are expended." This was no way to deal with the obstinate, professed witch-doctors who defied the doctrines and the discipline of the missionaries.[55]

The anonymous observer's comments reveal the intensity of the legalism that pervaded the period.[56] Precept 13 prohibited the employment of an Indian or *mulata* to serve in the Father's house; the intent of the precept was to remove all possibility of scandal that the missionaries might violate their vows of chastity and the rule of celibacy, as well as obviate any temptation that might have arisen. But the precept, as stated, seemed to preclude even the situation in which a maid servant might enter the Father's quarters to perform the customary "feminine" duties of cleaning, laundry, or making tortillas. The commentator felt it would be wiser to spell out the prohibition so that the maid servants would only be excluded from residing or sleeping within the Father's house. The work they did, however, should not be excluded. It would appear from the simplicity of the precept that the interpretation desired by the observer was indeed the desired effect of the restriction, but the climate of literal exactness seems to have demanded more precise formulation.[57]

The same tendency toward legal literalism was shown in a lengthy discussion the commentator wrote on the subject of *negocio* (or business for profit). The matter has always been a delicate one in the administration of temporal affairs by the Church. Business is by nature foreign to the declared purposes of religious convention. Nevertheless, religious ministers have found it necessary to engage in temporal affairs for their own survival, if not for the temporal advance of the people they serve. In the case of the northwestern missions the problem was acute and complicated by the tax free support of the Crown. Protective *cédulas* kept the Indian missions effectively free from encroachment by the ecclesiastical hierarchy and the provincial governors.

---

[53] ARSJ, *Misc. Mex.* IX, f. 400.
[54] Ibid.
[55] Ibid.
[56] In the mid-eighteenth century when the Society and the Church were beset by the later declared heresy of Jansenism, this serious issue was deferred in favor of deciding whether Coadjutor Brothers should have worn birettas and whether the birettas should have had three or four peaks.
[57] *Misc. Mex.* IX, f. 401.

Questions arose in the commentator's mind to what extent could the missions be permitted to remain exempt from diezmos and other taxes while simultaneously permitting the produce of the mission fields and the prescribed Indian labor to be sold at a profit? To whom was the profit to go? Could the profit be used by a missionary for any purpose he considered legitimate, or was it to be held exclusively for the use of enriching the mission church?

The commentator attacked the position that had been taken by Father Visitor Luis Lucas Alvarez who had ordered that *all* forms of business or profit-making were prohibited to the missions. Such a prohibition precluded the missionary from earning his own keep or assisting the pueblos. The observer argued for a clarification in the wording of the precepts so a mission could earn just recompense for legitimate produce; any purchase of goods or the sale of them for the pure purpose of making a profit was still to be prohibited. As for bartering, the missions simply were not able to avoid such practices because of the scarcity of valuable goods and money.[58] Quite frankly, the commentator held "little regard for precepts about business matters."[59] If the business involved sufficient sums, the offender would have sinned gravely against his vows anyway; if the sums were insignificant, the precepts only added unnecessary burdens. The simple horror of violating an ecclesiastical precept should have been ample enough to deter a worthy missionary from engaging in business.[60]

Following rather closely the recommendations of the anonymous observer, Father Provincial Andrés Xavier García issued a final set of precepts after receiving the approval of his consultors. The precepts were promulgated June 23, 1747.[61] Most of them expressed a cautious permissiveness. For example, the Bishops preferred Spaniards to pay fixed fees for funerals, but the missionaries were ordered not to charge anything, although they were allowed to accept whatever offerings the Spaniards might freely make. In any case, whatever was received as a funeral fee was to have been entered in church ledgers and applied to the church and not the ministers.[62] Whenever a donation was made for the adornment or rebuilding of a church, while debts were still outstanding, the money had to be deposited with a reputable layman, or the Rector of the mission district, so that no one could later charge any misappropriation of the gift.[63] The precept against knowing anything about mining was retained in all its simplicity; a missionary could not work at mining and he was forbidden to have even *indirect* knowledge

---

[58] Ibid., f. 401v. Alvarez had conceded that bartering was essential on the missions, but he still believed it had to be prohibited. Alvarez was contemporary to Balthasar, the presumed anonymous author.

[59] Ibid., f. 403v.

[60] Ibid.

[61] Part Two, p. 122. For Balthasar's intimate involvement see AHH, *Temp.* 1126, exp. 5 which is a letter to Father Cristóbal Escobar from San Gregorio, Jan. 16, 1747. García became provincial shortly after.

[62] Ibid. For a list of ecclesiastical fees see AGI, México, 61-3-14; cited in Pastells, *México* XXV, pp. 6-8.

[63] Ibid., Part Two, rule 2, p. 122.

of the science and art of mining.[64] Nothing could be solicited or accepted from a layman in order to sell it for profit, nor could a Father indebt himself to a layman for over 100 pesos, except in case of necessity or when the mission could easily repay the borrowed money.[65] And the perennial beggars were restricted to an alms of six pesos and encouraged to move on.

Garcia's "final precepts" set down specific rules regarding income and expense and the remittal of money to Mexico. No missionary could henceforth send any silver to any layman in Mexico; everything had to be sent to the Procurator or some other Jesuit. On the missions, itemized statements had to be kept on the income from cattle, sheep, horses, and so forth. And following the philosophy expressed in the "observaciones," Garcia changed the precept on punishment. Normally an Indian was not to receive more than six lashes, but more serious faults, at the discretion of the priest, could merit up to twenty-five lashes.

The last addition to the Garcia precepts reveals a new situation that had developed on the mission frontiers. The Fathers were reminded of the grave obligation they had to reside in their missions. They were not permitted to absent themselves except for serious reasons, and then only for brief periods.[66] Throughout the last half century of Jesuit missionary endeavor a frequent complaint was sounded that the Fathers were receiving stipends from the Royal Treasury for vacant missions, completely unattended by any missionaries. The vacant missions, in fact, were visited by the neighboring priests or the Father Visitor when he made his annual visitation. But the overall scarcity of missionaries and the greatly extended mission field had placed a heavy burden on the men in the field.

The rule on the semiannual junta illustrates the changed situation. The juntas were supposed to be held on Corpus Christi and on the Epiphany, but this regulation, perforce, removed the missionaries from their districts at a time which others felt should be reserved for major Indian festivals.[67] The earlier rules had stressed the protection of the spiritual welfare of the isolated missionary; the later rules shifted the emphasis to a continual care of a mission district very similar to a secular, parochial spirit. Garcia's instruction limited the number of Fathers attending a junta to three. The conference aspect of the junta had obviously dwindled to unimportance.

The anonymous observer's comments cast substantial light on the reasoning behind the limitation of the junta. The observer realized the reasons for the junta were weighty, but he favored the practice of the Fathers, which apparently ran counter to the rules.[68] Many legitimate reasons existed for absenting oneself from a district, but none of the justifications for absence

---

[64] Ibid., p. 122, rule 4.

[65] Ibid.; An account book of Manje shows Kino owed him 104 pesos, but this occurred prior to the issuance of the precept. See AHP, *Año* 1707 (University of Arizona Microfilm 318, frame 180sq.).

[66] Part Two, p. 124; addition 6a.

[67] Ibid., p. 69, Cabrero's Code of 1662. Corpus Christi was the more important feast; it falls on the Thursday after Trinity Sunday. The Epiphany falls on January 6.

[68] ARSJ, *Misc. Mex.* IX, f. 475.

solved the actual problems arising from the absence.[69] Pueblos often had no Mass on feast days; many of the faithful died without benefit of the sacraments while the priest was gone. The situation was not adequately answered by saying that a neighboring priest would minister to the dying or in case of need. Frequently the "near-by" Father would be twenty or thirty leagues distant. A partial solution, in the observer's opinion, would have been to permit each priest to celebrate two Masses daily, which was a custom not yet established in the Church.[70]

No one would rationally expect the extensive Jesuit mission system of northwestern New Spain to have operated according to a few, simple rules. Thus far, this study has reviewed only the major rules, instructions, and precepts that governed the system, but hundreds of letters of advice and exception have been omitted for the sake of generalization and clarity.[71] The depth of concern the missionaries felt for properly administering their missions would be difficult to portray; it is ubiquitous in the extant documentation. What this discussion has attempted to show is the growth and change in the administrative rules which acted as gauges in depicting the evolution of the apostolate. Rules and precepts define the limits of activity; they do not describe the activity itself. That activity is best studied by an analysis of the methods that constituted it.

---

[69] Ibid., the sufficient reasons for absence were: 1) the rules order such absence — for example, the juntas; 2) charity and public example are best served by convocations at festival times; 3) absence is necessary to receive interior guidance, exchanging cases of conscience, and for the manifestation of conscience (according to Rules of the Society); 4) Bishops, Governors, and major superiors require companionship on their visitations; 5) the missionary should console himself by getting together with companions to change his "air" (environment); 6) absence required for seeking alms and other necessities; 7) illness demands one leave or go to the assistance of another.

[70] Ibid., f. 475v.

[71] The personal letters of missionaries to Provincials, Procurators, Visitors, and fellow missionaries can be found in profusion in the archives of Mexico. Few of these "internal matters" were ever copied and sent on to official archives such as Seville.

The Rectorates, Cabeceras and Visitas, including founding dates, for the Mission Provinces of Sinaloa and Sonora of the Society of Jesus.

The Rectorate of San Felipe y Santiago
(under the administration of the College of Sinaloa)

Cabecera	Cabecera-Misión	Visitas
1) Toro	San Joseph de Toro, 1620	Santa Catarina de Baimena, 1620 San Ignacio de Chois, 1620 (frontier)
2) Vaca	La Concepción de Vaca, 1620	Santiago de Huites, 1620 (frontier)
3) Mochicahui	San Gerónimo de Mochicahui, 1614	San Miguel Ahome, 1614 Santa María Ahome, 1614
4) Tehueco	La Visitación de N.S. de Tehueco, 1614	La Asunción de N.S. de Sirivijoa, 1614 San Joseph de Charay, 1614
5) Guasave	San Pedro y Pablo de Guasave, 1590	Los Santos Reyes de Tamazula, 1590 N.P. San Ignacio de Nío, 1590
6) Bamoa	La Concepción de N.S. de Bamoa, 1590	San Lorenzo de Oquera, 1608
7) Mocorito	San Miguel de Mocorito, 1614	San Pedro de Bacoburito, 1614
8) Chicorato	N.S. de La Concepción de Chicorato, 1614	San Ignacio de los Chicuros, 1680
9) Ocoroni	Santiago de Ocoroni, 1590	

The Rectorate of Nuestro Padre San Ignacio de los Rios Yaqui y Mayo

1) Rahun	La Asunción de N.S. de Rahun, 1617	SS. Trinidad de Potám, 1617
2) Torím	N.P. San Ignacio de Torím, 1617	SS. Trinidad de Vicam, 1617
3) Bacum	Santa Rosa de Bacum, 1617	Espiritu Santo de Cocorit, 1617
4) Santa Cruz de Mayo	Santa Cruz de Mayo, 1614	San Juan de Tauer, 1614 Espiritu Santo de Echojoa, 1614
5) Navojoa	La Navidad de N.S. de Navojoa, 1614	La Concepción de N.S. de Corimpo, 1614
6) Tesia	N.P. San Ignacio de Tesia, 1614	Santa Catarina Martyr de Caimoa, 1614

The College and District of Tepahui also comes under the administration of the Mission of San Ignacio de Tesia:

La Asunción de N.S. de Tepahui, 1616
San Andrés Apóstol de Conicari, 1621
La Asunción de N.S. de Macoyahui, 1622

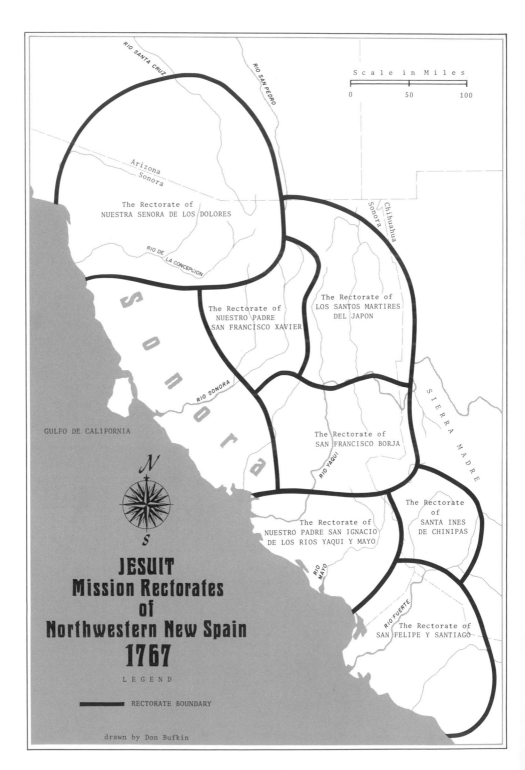

RIO SANTA CRUZ

RIO SAN PEDRO

Scale in Miles

0   50   100

Arizona
Sonora

The Rectorate of
NUESTRA SENORA DE LOS DOLORES

Sonora

Chihuahua

RIO DE LA CONCEPCION

S o n o r a

The Rectorate of
NUESTRO PADRE
SAN FRANCISCO XAVIER

The Rectorate of
LOS SANTOS MARTIRES
DEL JAPON

RIO SONORA

GULFO DE CALIFORNIA

The Rectorate of
SAN FRANCISCO BORJA

SIERRA MADRE

RIO YAQUI

N

S

The Rectorate of
NUESTRO PADRE SAN IGNACIO
DE LOS RIOS YAQUI Y MAYO

The Rectorate
of
SANTA INES
DE CHINIPAS

RIO MAYO

JESUIT
Mission Rectorates
of
Northwestern New Spain
1767

LEGEND

RIO FUERTE

The Rectorate of
SAN FELIPE Y SANTIAGO

RECTORATE BOUNDARY

drawn by Don Bufkin

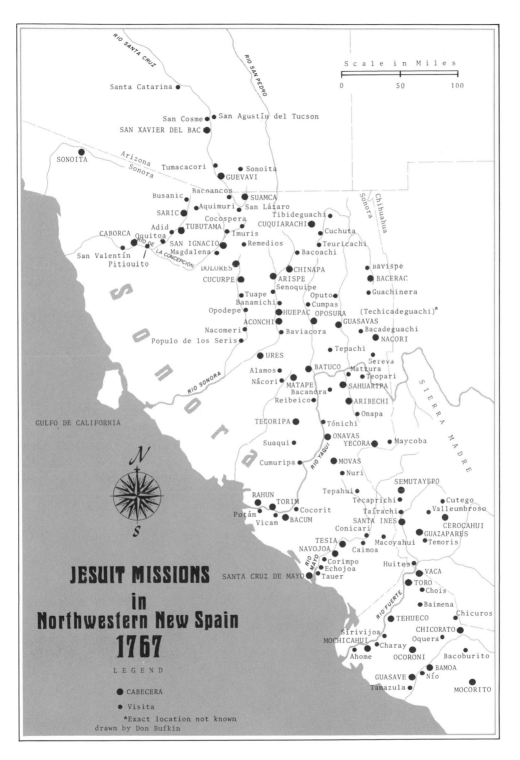

Scale in Miles

0   50   100

RIO SANTA CRUZ

RIO SAN PEDRO

Santa Catarina

San Cosme   San Agustín del Tucson

SAN XAVIER DEL BAC

SONOITA   Arizona   Tumacacori   Sonoita

Sonora   GUEVAVI

Bacoancos

Busanic   SUAMCA

Aquimuri   San Lázaro

SARIC   Cocospera   Tibideguachi

Adid   TUBUTAMA   CUQUIARACHI   Cuchuta

CABORCA   Oquitoa   Imuris

San Valentín   SAN IGNACIO   Remedios   Teuricachi

Pitiquito   Magdalena   Bacoachi

RIO DE LA CONCEPCION

DOLORES

CUCURPE   CHINAPA   Bavispe

ARISPE   BACERAC

Senoquipe

Tuape   Oputo   Guachinera

Banamichi   Cumpas

Opodepe   HUEPAC OPOSURA   (Techicadeguachi)*

ACONCHI   GUASAVAS

Nacomeri   Baviacora   Bacadeguachi

Populo de los Seris   NACORI

Tepachi

URES

Alamos   BATUCO   Sereva

Nácori   Matzura

MATAPE   Teopari

Bacanora   SAHUARIPA

Reibeico   ARIBECHI

Onapa

TECORIPA   Tónichi

Sunqui   ONAVAS

GULFO DE CALIFORNIA   YECORA   Maycoba

Cumuripa   MOVAS

Nuri

Tepahui   SEMUTAYEPO

RAHUN   Tecaprichi   Cutego

TORIM   Tairachi   Valleumbroso

Potám   Cocorit   SANTA INES   CEROCAHUI

Vicam   BACUM   Conicari   GUAZAPARES

Macoyahui   Temoris

TESIA   Caimoa

NAVOJOA

Corimpo   Huites   VACA

Echojoa

SANTA CRUZ DE MAYO   Tauer   TORO

Chois

Baimena

TEHUECO   Chicuros

Sirivijoa   CHICORATO

MOCHICAHUI   Charay   Oquera

Ahome   OCORONI   Bacoburito

GUASAVE   BAMOA

Tamazula   Nío   MOCORITO

SIERRA MADRE

Chihuahua Sonora

RIO SONORA

RIO YAQUI

RIO MAYO

RIO FUERTE

JESUIT MISSIONS
in
Northwestern New Spain
1767

The Rectorate of Santa Inés de Chínipas, Province of Sinaloa

Cabecera	Cabecera-Misión	Visitas
1) Santa Inés	Santa Inés de Guairopa, 1676	N.S. de Guadalupe de Taírachi, 1676
2) Guazapares	Santa Teresa de Guazapares, 1676	Santa María Magdalena de Temoris, 1676 N.S. de Valleumbroso, 1677
3) Semutayepo	N.S. de Loreto de Semutayepo, 1678	Santa Ana de Tecaprichi, 1678
4) Cerocahui	San Francisco Xavier de Cerocahui, 1678	Los Santos Mártires del Japon de Cutego, 1678

The Rectorate of San Francisco Borja, Province of Sonora

Cabecera	Cabecera-Misión	Visitas
1) Onavas	N.P. San Ignacio de Onavas, 1622	Santa María del Populo de Tónichi, 1628
2) Movas	Santa María de Movas, 1622	Santa Ana de Nuri, 1622
3) Tecoripa	San Francisco Borja de Tecoripa, 1619	San Pedro de Cumuripa, 1619 N.P. San Ignacio de Suaqui
4) Sahuaripa	N.S. de los Angeles de Sahuaripa, 1627	San Mateo de Matzura, 1674 San Joseph de Teopari, 1676
5) Aribechi	San Francisco Xavier de Aribechi, 1627	San Ignacio de Bacanora, 1627 Santa Rosalía de Onapa, 1677
6) Mátape	San Joseph de Mátape, 1629	Santa Cruz de Nácori, 1629 La Asunción de N.S. de los Alamos, 1629 San Francisco Xavier de Reibeico, 1673
7) Yécora	San Ildefonso de Yécora, 1673	San Francisco de Borja de Maycoba, 1676

The Rectorate of Nuestro Padre San Francisco Xavier, Province of Sonora

Cabecera	Cabecera-Misión	Visitas
1) Cucurpe	Los Santos Reyes Magos de Cucurpe, 1647	San Miguel de Tuape, 1647 La Asunción de N.S. de Opodepe, 1649
2) Ures	San Miguel de los Ures, 1636	N.S. del Rosario de Nacomeri, 1638 N.S. del Populo de los Seris, 1679
3) Aconchi	San Pedro de Aconchi, 1639	N.S. de la Concepción de Baviacora, 1639
4) Huepac	San Lorenzo de Huepac, 1639	N.S. de los Remedios de Banámichi, 1639 N.P. San Ignacio de Senoquipe, 1646
5) Arizpe	N.S. de la Asunción de Arizpe, 1648	
6) Chinapa	San Joseph de Chinapa, 1648	San Miguel de Bacoachi, 1650

[36]

The Rectorate of Los Santos Mártires del Japon, Province of Sonora

Cabecera	Cabecera-Misión	Visitas
1) Guasavas	San Francisco Xavier de Guasavas, 1645	N.P. San Ignacio de Oputo, 1645 Santa Gertrudis de Techicadeguachi, 1645
2) Batuco	N.S. de la Asunción de Batuco, 1629	San Francisco Xavier de Batuco, 1629 San Joaquín y Santa Ana de Tepachi, 1636
3) Nácori	Santa María de Nácori, 1645	San Luis Gonzaga de Bacadeguachi, 1645 San Tomás Apóstol de Sereva, 1645
4) Bacerac	N.S. de la Asunción de Bacerac, 1645	San Miguel Bavispe, 1645 San Juan Evangelista de Guachinera, 1645
5) Cuquiárachi	N.P. San Ignacio de Cuquiárachi, 1653	San Francisco Xavier de Cuchuta, 1653 N.S. de Guadalupe de Teuricachi, 1653 Santa Rosa de Tibideguachi, 1653
6) Oposura	San Miguel Arcángel de Oposura, 1644	N.S. de la Asunción de Cumpas, 1644

The Rectorate of Nuestra Señora de los Dolores

1) Dolores	N.S. de los Dolores de Cosari, 1687	N.S. de los Remedios de Doagibubig, 1687 N.S. del Pilar y Santiago de Cocóspera, 1687
2) San Ignacio	N.P. San Ignacio de Caburica, 1687	Santa María de Magdalena, 1687 San José de los Imuris, 1687
3) Tubutama	San Pedro y Pablo de Tubutama, 1689	Santa Teresa del Adid, 1689 San Antonio del Oquitoa, 1689
4) Caborca	N.S. de La Purísima Concepción de Caborca, 1689	San Diego del Pitiquito, 1689 San Valentín de Busanic, 1691
5) Saric	Santa Gertrudis del Saric, 1689	San Bernardo de Aquimuri, 1689 San Ambrosio del Búsanic y Tucubavia, 1698
6) Sonoita	San Marcelo de Sonoita, 1697	
7) Guevavi	Los Santos Angeles de Guevavi, 1691	Los Santos Reyes de Sonoita, 1691 San Cayetano del Tumacacori, 1691
8) Suamca	Santa María de Suamca, 1689	San Lázaro, 1689 San Luis de Bacoancos, 1689
9) Bac	San Xavier del Bac, 1692	San Cosme del Tucson, 1692 Santa Catarina del Cuytoabagum, 1699

The founding dates as given are the dates when baptisms were first given in the villages. The actual construction of churches at missions and visitas is unreliable and misleading in establishing the age of Christian communities. With the exception of the Rectorate of Nuestra Señora de los Dolores in the Pimería Alta the above listings were made by Father Visitor Juan de Almonacír in 1685. The document is preserved in the Archivo Histórico de Hacienda, Ramo Temporalidades, Legajo 1126, Expediente 4.

[37]

The massive ruins of San José del Batuco give witness to the progress and decline of frontier history in Sonora.

Jesuit Mission Methodology

 issiology in the seventeenth and eighteenth centuries had not yet been reduced to a science. The methods the missionaries employed were essentially pragmatic responses to situations as perceived. But the perception of the missionary in the field was not always keen or subtle. Although the flare for conquest diminished in the later Spanish empire, the primary goals of expansion and conversion still remained fundamental forces in Spanish colonization. The weightier problems came with the consolidation of the geographic and religious gains, and more consistent methods developed that seemed consonant with the principles by which the New World was governed.

In many ways the Spanish approach was less concerned with methodology than with the introduction of institutional structures that would impose acceptable cultural patterns. As earlier shown in this study, the documentation for institutional rule is very much in evidence, but a similar body of material for methodology is almost unknown. No historians have discovered a "manual for missions," nor is such a manual mentioned in the mainstream of the literature. Methodology for the Jesuit missions is something that has to be reconstructed from an analysis of extant mission documents. It seems true to assert that the concern for discovering a methodology pertains more to modern scholars who have made a science of culture than to the historical persons who shaped it.[1]

The fundamental objective of all missionary endeavor was the religious conversion of the nonbelieving native. Whatever helped toward that goal was utilized as fully and extensively as possible. Hence, the shift in approach from itinerant mission bands to resident missionaries constituted a change in methodology. Conversion was considered more complete and permanent when missionaries were present to prevent a reversion to old cultural habits.

In all these processes the missionaries persisted in their primary focus on religious practices. The reducción of an Indian tribe certainly involved

---

[1] The only known and extant material that qualifies as a manual of methodology pertains to the direction of haciendas by Jesuit Brothers. See Francois Chavalier, editor, *Instrucciones a los hermanos jesuitas administradores de haciendas;* this is the edited version of the manuscript found in AHH, *Temp.* 258, exp. 9. For comparison see Pablo Macero, *Instrucciones para el manejo de las haciendas jesuitas del Perú* (Lima: Universidad Nacional Mayor de San Marcos, 1966). Some methodology can be gleaned from P. José de Acosta, *Historia natural y moral de las Indias.*

acculturation techniques, but the conscious purpose of the mission was less to introduce a new culture than to remove obstacles to the acceptance of religious doctrine. This explains the preponderance in mission literature of concerns for effective indoctrination, baptism, and participation in religious ceremony.

It should be remembered that all the Jesuit missions of New Spain were established after the Council of Trent (1545–1563). Although the Council was held towards the end of the era of discovery, no formal sessions were devoted to the problem of cultural adaptation or to the introduction of the Christian faith among distinct and variant culture groups. The stress in the Roman Church at the time was on doctrinal purity and conformity to Roman tradition. In the mission apostolate there was no question about cultural variation; conversion presupposed the total acceptance of Christian dogma and Greco-Roman culture. The doctrine was to be learned thoroughly; the rituals were to be observed exactly; Christians were to be Christians everywhere in the world. Hardly any attention was paid to the possible validity of a meta-cultural approach to the Christian faith.[2]

Sources for the study of mission methodology are comparatively scarce. The writings of Father José de Acosta on the history and nature of the Indians of Peru are a well-known source for insights into sixteenth-century mission theory.[3] Comparable to these for northern Mexico are the works by Father Andrés Pérez de Ribas, who lived as a missionary in Sinaloa and later held the position of Provincial for New Spain (1637–1640). Pérez de Ribas' frequently quoted Historia de los triunphos de nuestra santa fee provides regional histories of the establishment and early development of the northern Mexican missions. Book Seven of that work begins a generalized discussion of the Indians and their openness to the Gospel. Curiously, in the Roman archives of the Society of Jesus there is a manuscript of fifty-nine folio pages entitled Libro séptimo de algunos puntos dignos de notar en la Historia de las missiones de la Compañia de Jesús en Nueva España, en particular de la de Cinaloa.[4] The manuscript is located with several partial writings of Pérez de Ribas. Internal evidence of the Libro séptimo manuscript shows this, too, is a previously unknown and unpublished text by that same author.[5]

The manuscript is unique inasmuch as it discusses the means or methods

---

[2] "Meta-cultural" is the term used by Antonio da Silva, Trent's Impact on the Portuguese Patronage Missions, cf. p. 25. A significant finding of Silva's study is Trent's silence on missiology and acculturation.

[3] P. José de Acosta, Historia natural y moral de las Indias; several editions have appeared in Spanish, French, and English. For an analysis of Acosta's missiology, compared with Thomas of Jesus, see Ronan Hoffman, Pioneer Theories of Missiology (Washington, D.C.: Catholic University of America Press, 1960).

[4] P. Andrés Pérez de Ribas, Libro Séptimo, ARSJ, Mex. 19, ff. 131-190v.

[5] Ibid., f. 178v. Speaking of himself, the author says "he lived sixteen years among these Indians," and that he visited Father Bernardo Cisneros "only two months before he was killed." He also spent twelve years with the Marquis of Guadalajara in Mexico. This fits Pérez exactly, and he mentions the same events in the same way in P. Andrés Pérez de Ribas, Historia de los triunfos de nuestra Santa Fee entre gentes las mas barbaras y fieras del nuevo orbe. Translated and abridged by Tomás Robertson; published as My Life Among the Savage Nations of New Spain, Book II, Chapter 11.

(*medios*) by which abundant fruits can be reaped in missionary labors. What is perhaps more revealing, in the context of mission methodology, is the consciousness the writer has of the changes that happen in native peoples by their acceptance of baptism. His entire method reduces to the employment of means whereby the natives will accept Christian doctrine that in itself will transform the pagans into responsible vassals of the king. More explicitly, methodology in the mind of the missionary is summarized by the working of Divine grace; this was a full and adequate explanation for the religiously oriented man of colonial Spain. What would be called methods or means by a twentieth-century analyst are no more than those procedures and momentary insights that worked to bring about faith and its transformations. What, then, were the stages of those transformations? It might be best to follow the discussion of Pérez de Ribas.

He attributed the profound changes in the Indians to the grace of baptism. The Indians displayed a more pacific behavior as a direct result of their acceptance of the sacrament. Secondly, he felt the disappearance of the Indians' "ancient" addiction to intoxicating beverages proved that religious conversion wrought profound changes. Only after a lengthy assertion that religious and social change results from sacramental causes does Pérez de Ribas descend to the plane of pure methodology.[6]

The first step by which the Fathers "win over the pagan nations and dispose the people to receive the Gospel" is made when the Indians come to the Fathers and ask for baptism. At this time they promise "to gather themselves into pueblos from their rancherías even before the Father arrives" so he can more easily teach them Christian doctrine.[7] The Indians making the petition were publicly enrolled before the Captain of the Presidio, who held the power to punish falsifiers. Then, the Fathers offered the Indian chiefs various trinkets that they valued, all the while insisting on a peaceful reception.[8]

Sometimes the sons of the chiefs were accepted by the missionary and subsequently sent on to seminaries established in the mission province. The older boys learned the doctrine and eventually returned home to assist the resident missionaries in teaching. Frequently the Indians were taught to play musical instruments "at which they were very talented." Such students usually proved the most faithful, along with their families, during rebellions and disturbances.[9]

When the first entradas were made among the native peoples, the Fathers were ordinarily met about one or two leagues outside the pueblo. The reception party travelled along paths cleaned up for the occasion and went directly to the ramada-chapel where the Fathers preached about the purpose of their coming. While the Indians were seated, the priests explained how they had come from far across the sea to bring news of the Gospel of salvation.[10]

---

[6] Ibid., ff. 131-135v.
[7] Ibid., ff. 133 and 136. Contrast this to the claims of force.
[8] Ibid., f. 136v.
[9] Ibid., f. 137.
[10] Ibid., ff. 139-139v. Kino followed the same technique; cf. *Memoirs*, Book I, Chap. 4.

Following this sermon, the Father accepted any children offered for baptism; normally the children were between two and seven years of age. Seldom were older children admitted to the baptismal ceremony because they fled out of fear if they were even invited.[11]

The mothers and children would be seated in a large circle, grouped according to their pueblos of origin. It was not unusual to have two or three hundred children so situated. The Father wrote down the names of the children in the book of baptisms that he always carried with him. If he failed to do this with exactness, it became impossible to identify the persons when they later presented themselves for marriage or confirmation — not to mention that the Indians often forgot their Christian names because they were so new. "The Father could not remember all of them."[12] First, the names were registered in the book, then the baptismal ceremony followed. If the Father was not diligent in setting down the children's names to be baptized, he would often find that the mother and child had left the chapel for some reason, such as to bathe in the nearby river to cool off in the heat.

Christian doctrine was always taught in the Indians' native language. In order not to impede the learning of the doctrine, Mass was celebrated very early in the morning so sufficient time would remain for the Indians to perform their daily tasks — working in the fields, hunting, and so forth. The signal for Mass, hopefully, was the ringing of a bell, but often no bell was available so the *caciques* (chiefs) roamed the pueblo shouting with voices that "their guardian angels fortified and that struck fear into the devil."[13] Pérez de Ribas noted that the Indians liked the sound of a bell, even if small.[14]

The purpose of an established mission was the teaching of catechism or Christian doctrine, for which reason the mission was legally classified as a doctrina. By rule, as has been shown, the doctrine was taught twice daily to children; adults were only expected to be present once a day, normally in the morning.[15] When the Indians were assembled in the church or at the ramada, men and women sat separately on each side of the altar while the children sat in front and around the altar. The doctrina was conducted by the Father if he was in the pueblo; if not, it was conducted by a *temastian* (catechist) who knew the catechism well enough to ask questions of the others. In the Father's absence the temastians also conducted the regular prayer services; this was also enjoined by rule.[16]

As the Indians became more proficient in the doctrine, which Pérez de Ribas claims the Indians did as well as any ancient Christians, the temastians would conduct examinations, asking the respondents to reply in words other than those memorized to show that they truly understood the lesson. After several days of such recitation and examination, the better qualified children

---

[11] Pérez de Ribas, *Libro Séptimo*, f. 139v.

[12] Ibid., f. 139v.

[13] Ibid., f. 142.

[14] Ibid. Among the Yaqui pueblos the Fathers had Indians carry the bells on their shoulders. These were hung on trees next to the chapel. The Indians were so pleased with the bells they often asked that they never be taken away.

[15] Part Two, p. 68, rule 11.

[16] Pérez de Ribas, *Libro Séptimo*, f. 143; also Part Two, p. 62, rule 6 and p. 63, rule 10.

and adults appealed to the *fiscal* (official church secretary) or the Father for admission to baptism. Then, the Father examined the candidates to determine whether any impediments barred them from receiving the sacrament; in the case of adults, this often involved the resolution of complex marriage relations. The Indians who qualified attended instructions morning and evening for eight days, at which times the obligations of the Christian Faith were explained in detail. For several days these candidates were set apart before Mass as in the case of the catechumens in the early Church.[17]

The missionary approach to marriage, as explained by Pérez de Ribas, was different from the way the role of the sacrament has often been described. Marriage customs among the various northern tribes differed among themselves, and all of them were at variance with the monogamous practice of the Roman Catholic Church. The missionaries insisted on sound instruction regarding the indissolubility of matrimony. Indissolubility needed careful explanation because the Indians feared that Christian marriage would encroach on their liberty to take the person they desired as their mate. If baptism required that they recognize as a mate someone to whom they had been married as a child, the Indians felt this could be undesirable, especially since they frequently exchanged partners.

Children were married in the Indian culture by "natural contract" at eight or ten years of age, although there was no cohabitation until the time of the official ceremony. If, on the other hand, a child was baptized when two or three years old, then the legitimacy of a later childhood marriage could be questioned. So, the missionaries carefully explained to the parents the difficulties that might result from their acceptance of Christianity for their child. At the same time, however, they taught that Christian marriage brought a stability to these relationships that the Indians had never experienced. Christian charity was a better guarantee of marital love than familiar Indian customs. Clearly, the methodology regarding marriage did not involve a harsh legal insistence, but rather a staunch persuasion on the value of a firm union contracted as a consenting adult.[18]

Confession among the Indians was made annually during Lent. The Fathers had to make certain the confession was integral, that is, that the penitent truly confessed all his sins according to number and kind, which was strictly enjoined by the Council of Trent.[19] The Tridentine regulation had a literate population in mind, and the universal, ecclesiastical law made it difficult for missionaries among illiterate peoples to feel they had satisfied the desires of the Church. The Fathers frequently preached on the necessity for an integral confession and stressed the proper inventory of sins. The Indians generally kept track of their sins on small knotted cords which they presented to the Father in confession, telling him that their sins were so many. In the beginning the Indians were instructed to tell the Father that

---

[17] *Libro Séptimo,* ff. 143-143v.
[18] Ibid., f. 144-144v.
[19] See Council of Trent, Session XIV, canon 4; cf. Denzinger-Schonmetzer, *Enchiridion Symbolorum: Definitionum et Declarationum,* no. 917.

they did not wish to omit any sins, so they handed over the whole cord. With the priest's absolution they understood they were free of all their sins.[20]

Actually the priests were not as sophisticated or demanding as European orthodoxy might have demanded. Confessional procedure took the uncultured ways of the Indians into consideration. Making a comparison to the *Acts of the Apostles* (Chapter 19, verse 19) where the magicians at Ephesus burned their books, Pérez de Ribas remarked that the Indians had no books to burn, but they threw figurines of serpents and fish into bonfires to rid themselves of connections with demons.[21] Unquestionably the Fathers were anxious to eradicate the influence of the *hechicheros* (medicine men), but instead of eliminating these competitors by force, the Fathers preferred to beat them at what the Indians probably felt was their own game.

Although many instances of conflict between the priests and medicine men are recorded, there is no evidence that a precise method was ever employed to counteract these tribal leaders. To the contrary, it appears that the missionaries only cautiously discredited the role of the tribal medicine men. Natural disasters, such as the death of a person from lightning or a tragic flood, were associated with antecedent rituals performed by hechicheros. Many early missions were established at Indian pueblos that doubled as ceremonial centers. Rather than select a neighboring site to compete against Indian religious ritual, the missionaries would erect a church and house in the same village, thus hoping to challenge traditional religion head-on.[22]

Pérez de Ribas frequently mentioned the presence and influence of tribal magicians, but the response of the priests toward them was not one of open belligerence. The priests hoped even for their eventual conversion. Kino spoke of the medicine men at Remedios and described how he painstakingly argued against their claims.[23] And in an *informe* for 1745 Father Gaspar Stiger, the superior at San Ignacio in the Pimería Alta, described the school for medicine men located at San Xavier del Bac. Although Stiger was irritated at their continual activity, he made no concerted effort to eradicate the practices.[24] Generally speaking, mission literature supports the conclusion that the missionaries were reluctantly tolerant of the medicine men and seldom played the role of a puritanical firebrand.

Despite the fact that the sixteenth- and seventeenth-century missionaries theoretically embraced an enlightened religious doctrine, they shared in principle some of the same attitudes that motivated the medicine men. Indian superstition was cast as demonology; their ritual practices stemmed less from ignorance than from an association with diabolical powers. The great difference between the hechicheros and the Spanish priests was the source of their power over natural and human phenomena. As Enlightenment ideas began to influence religious thought and practice, the superstitious rituals of the

---

[20] Pérez de Ribas, *Libro Séptimo*, f. 159v.
[21] Ibid., f. 160.
[22] Examples of missions at ceremonial pueblos are: Onabas, Mátape, Ures, Remedios, Imuris, Oquitoa, and Bac.
[23] Kino, *Memoirs*, Vol. I, p. 114.
[24] Stiger, *Informe de la Misión del San Ignacio*, 1745, Mateu Collection, Barcelona. Photo copy available, ARSJ.

medicine men ceased to retain the color of witchcraft and were looked on as the empty ceremony of ignorant men who blocked progress. There was no evolution in the methodology of handling medicine-men competitors; the evolution came in attitudes toward this class of Indian leader. A breakdown in tolerance toward them is evidenced in the closing years of Jesuit mission activity.[25] Strangely enough, the rigors of Jansenism penetrated the thought of the eighteenth century and subtly fashioned a superstitious legalism out of Trent's decrees which has persisted even into the twentieth century. Once the demons were dead, superstition was pitted against superstition in the Western mind.

Besides the *Libro séptimo* of Pérez de Ribas, only one other contemporary document consciously generalizes about mission methodology, at least the only one known to be extant.[26] This document comprises Book Eight of Kino's *Vida del F. X. Saeta.* In eulogizing the protomartyr of the Pimería Alta, Kino outlined his own theory as if they were sayings of the fallen Saeta. This portion of Kino's writings has been passed over because it perhaps appears on the surface to be pious aphorisms.

Kino placed full stress on the character of the missionary as the primary means to achieve success in converting the Indian. In this regard he closely resembles Pérez de Ribas. Like Pérez de Ribas, Kino dwelled on the need for the missionary to excel in the virtue of patience — not only because the Indians were often too slow to adapt, but also because the living conditions were hardly comparable to the comforts known to the cultured men of Europe. Close, personal contact with the Indian was an essential in any successful program of change or conversion; there was no magic set of techniques that of itself could bring about either. Kino had no place for priests who stood on their dignity, teaching doctrine to the Indians as from a platform of authority. Conversions are "neither well nor sufficiently achieved when one sits perched on his chair ordering subordinates or Indian officials to do what he (the missionary) should be doing personally by sitting down time and again with them on earthen floors or on a rock."[27]

Kino and Pérez de Ribas both allude to the necessary relations missionaries must have with the Spanish military garrisons. Each drew on his own experience. Pérez de Ribas glowed warmly over the valor and prudence of Don Diego Martínez de Hurdaide, who substantially assisted the expansion of the early Jesuit missions in Sinaloa and southern Sonora.[28] Kino lauded the military only generically; he emphasized the need for soldiers "of discre-

---

[25] Cf. Henry F. Dobyns, *Pioneering Christians Among the Perishing Indians of Tucson,* p. 11.

[26] None of the several contemporary works about mission life in northwestern New Spain attempted to theorize about the proper conduct of the missionary in the field. The classic *Rudo Ensayo* of Father Juan Nentwig gives an excellent description of the mission territory and living circumstances. The *Apostólicos Afanes* of Father José Ortega presents only an historical account of the origin and development of several mission areas. The diaries and accounts of Fathers Ignaz Pfefferkorn, Jacob Baegart, and Joseph Och are post-expulsion (1767) reflections on missions, mission life, and the general environment of New Spain.

[27] Cf. Polzer-Burrus, *Kino's Biography,* p. 187.

[28] Pérez de Ribas, *Libro Séptimo,* f. 169sq.

tion" especially in places where there was no "firm government." Twice in
his missionary career Kino's work was spoiled by impetuous soldiers who
found a ready answer in sword or cannon. He was never prepared to accept
a claim that soldiers would make peace without treachery — of course, a
recent massacre was before his mind when he expounded these cautions.
Nonetheless, these cautions expressed the reasonable concern a missionary
needed to control Indian-military relations.[29] The burden both missionary-
historians placed on the shoulders of the Fathers was a far cry from piety;
it was an appeal for a Renaissance man.

Yet, this was not exactly Kino's position. For him the missionary had to
"handle new conversions with a genuine knack, being capable of accepting
suffering while he works hard and maintains a sense of tolerance." Indeed,
these qualities were "more valuable than other human talents, skills, sophis-
tication, eloquence, ingenuity, or advanced and subtle science."[30] Such an
attitude, so forcefully expressed by this seventeenth-century missionary,
again confirms the reason for a lack of mission manuals: God's grace and
Christian folly were the sufficient means to achieve lasting conversion and
change. Kino's methodology, it might be said, did not distinguish between
method and motivation. The same tendency is visible in Pérez de Ribas, thus
giving substance to the contention that every means possible was employed
as long as it was primarily controlled by Christian virtue, especially charity.[31]

Perhaps one of the more effective adjuncts to the mission method was
the sheer joy-of-living approach that characterized mission activity. In Kino's
enthusiastic words:

> The greatness of new missions will shine not only in the eternity of
> heaven, but also in the most desolate and remote regions of the world.
> It will live on in the splendid construction of temples, churches, build-
> ings and houses. It will reflect in the solemnities of the saints, in gay
> fiestas, and in the treats of religious banquets; it will be heard in music
> and the choirs of singers. It will be seen in the bountiful spiritual and
> temporal wealth of opulent missions which, with reason, will be a source
> of pride.[32]

Comparing this euphoric vision of mission life with the calendar of regulated
feasts, it would appear that the missionaries were engaged in a continual
social whirl keyed to liturgical celebration.[33] The truth of the matter was
that the missionaries esteemed song, dance, and celebration as an effective
means to teach Christian doctrine.

---

[29] The murder of some Indians at La Paz, Baja California, in 1683 was not forgotten
and the recent killing at El Tupo rankled Kino; cf. Polzer-Burrus, *Kino's Biography,* pp. 135
and 193.

[30] Ibid., p. 193.

[31] The stress intended here is that mission methodology was essentially pragmatic
as long as the methods were firmly grounded in Christian charity. No inference is intended
regarding the bromide about the Jesuits that "the end justifies the means."

[32] Polzer-Burrus, *Kino's Biography,* pp. 215-216.

[33] For a calendar of sung Masses, processions, and vespers see Part Two of this text,
p. 78.

Indians were fascinated by and talented in the ways of music and dance. Even if the Indian only sang the Christian doctrine as a mere song, he was still exercising himself in the teachings of the Church. Small choirs and bands with stringed instruments formed the core of village pride even before the church may have been completed. Normally the musicians were younger natives open to the novelties of Spanish culture. The missionary realized these social activities provided both means and ends in involving previously warring factions to cooperate or compete in peaceful enterprises.[34] Life at a mission was not all song and dance, but nearly every acceptable means of social organization was employed in the search for wider cohesion beyond the confines of single tribes.

If mission methodology is defined as a patterned procedure to achieve the goals of a mission, then, logically, the methods used will reflect the changes in the mission situation. If the mission system was, indeed, evolving, as has been suggested, then the methods also underwent evolutionary change. This question is best studied by investigating the stages of mission growth.

Generally speaking, these stages can be classified according to 1) a pre-mission phase (or *entrada*), 2) a mission phase (or *conversión*), 3) a doctrinal or pre-parochial phase (or *doctrina*), and 4) the secularization phase (or *parroquia*). Methodology in the earlier phases is much more distinct and discernible. Methodology in the later stages converges with traditional pastoral practices and techniques.

Missionaries were not free agents in the plan of Spanish colonial expansion. Whatever advances they attempted in opening new missions had to be approved by both religious and civil authorities. Usually the prospective missionary accompanied a military patrol on a reconaissance of the territory where the tribe to be evangelized lived. The missionary's task was to show the more attractive aspects of Spanish culture, including the benefits of conversion, to the Indians. He presented them with gewgaws, trinkets, pieces of clothing, grains, and hardtack. All kinds of material goods were highly prized by the Indians, but gifts of real value were withheld during the pre-mission phase because of the high cost and because these rewards were given much later, after the acceptance of Christianity, vassalage to the King, and some signs of social stability.

Whenever an infant was offered for baptism, the missionary welcomed the opportunity to save its soul and lay the groundwork for relationships that would bind the infant and its parents ever so loosely with the Church. One missionary commented to the Opata of the Sonora River valley that whichever Father baptized a child also baptized its father, a comment that "astonished everyone." [35] Because of ecclesiastical restrictions, missionaries were not permitted to baptize adults without full instruction unless the adult was near death.[36]

---

[34] Pérez de Ribas, *Libro Séptimo*, ff. 132-132v.
[35] Cf. *Relación que sucede*, anonymous manuscript circa 1665, AHH, *Temp.* 1126, exp. 2.
[36] Cf. ARSJ, *Mex.* 17, f. 412; Salvatierra cautions on baptism.

The *entradas* (expeditions) served the purpose of introducing the missionary to a new people as well as allowing him to establish certain sacramental links with the Indians. During the circuit of the territory there was ample opportunity to observe language differences and ideal sites for the establishment of visitas or a cabecera. After the entrada was completed, it was possible to decide whether to recommend new missions or to entice, or even coerce, the Indians to leave their lands and join an established mission center.[37]

Once an entrada had been completed, the foundation of one or more missions was not guaranteed. Insistent and continual invitations were awaited before sending a priest to work in a new nation. Over the years a pattern emerged for Indians requesting a resident missionary to build a small chapel and house. But this did not certify that a missionary would come because that decision more often than not depended on Spanish expansionist designs. The scarcity of priests sometimes created fierce competition among the Indians to win the distinction of having a resident Father. This did not always work out peaceably, as in the case of the Pima rebellion in the Altar Valley in 1695 when the long awaited priest was assigned to Caborca instead of Oquitoa.[38] The site for a new mission was not always left in the hands of religious authorities; the civil authorities wielded great influence over the selection and timing of establishing new centers.[39]

In the initial encounters with Indians during an entrada, it is interesting to note that Pérez de Ribas, Kino, and Salvatierra, among others, used the device of maps to explain how far they had come to bring the news of salvation. Drawing crude maps or displaying world maps apparently astonished the Indians, who felt the priests came from another world.[40]

Added to this "other-world" impression was the missionaries' ability, together with the military escorts, to command the obedience of large and powerful animals. This phenomenon was noted during the conquest of Tenochtitlan (Mexico City), but the notion that Spaniards on horseback were gods was rapidly dispelled when the Aztecs learned that the Spaniards were as vulnerable as any other human being. Indian amazement, however, persisted throughout the frontier until the Indians lost their reverential fear of both Spaniards and animals by handling and possessing livestock.[41]

Spanish proclivity for paintings and statuary was well adapted for the pre-mission phase. Despite the cumbersome nature of such things missionaries carried them everywhere, introducing them to the natives as sacred objects. The Fathers realized this practice bordered on idolatry, but they were wise enough to understand that an intermediate level was necessary in the transfer of religious veneration from demonolatrical objects to monotheistic faith. Pictures and statues also identified a sacred area for the Indians

---

[37] Cf. Vincente Aguilar to Leonardo Xarino (Jatino), Ures, Aug. 7, 1640; AHH, *Temp.* 278, exp. 55.

[38] Polzer-Burrus, *Kino's Biography*, p. 83.

[39] Cf. Captain Antonio de Barba to the Visitor, Tuape, September 14, 1686; AHH, *Temp.* 278, exp. 52.

[40] Pérez de Ribas, *Libro Séptimo*, f. 139-139v; also Kino; *Memoirs*, Book One, Chap. 4.

[41] Cf. Kino, *Memoirs*, Vol. I, pp. 314-315.

who needed to understand Spanish insistence on the holiness of a church and its attendant buildings.

The interplay between the entering missionary and the receiving natives is fascinating. The Spaniards, carrying outward signs of their religious purpose — distinctive garb, sacred images, and crosses — always seem to respond favorably to their reception by the Indians who met them on the road with arches of flowers and large crosses. In ways, these were ceremonial games enacted by peoples of different cultures preparatory to further, more substantial cultural exchange.[42]

The baptism of infants and sick adults forged strong spiritual links between the Indians of a new region and the missionary. Similarly, the distribution of "canes of office" by the civil-military authorities achieved relationships between Indian rulers and Spanish government. Usually the Spaniards selected only recognized caciques as recipients of these official symbols of authority. Sometimes canes were bestowed on particularly cooperative Indians although they may have had no tribal standing. Indians who responded quickly to an acceptance of the Faith were rewarded with responsibilities of fiscales (petty officials) who supervised the church or church goods in the pueblo. Those who learned the doctrine very well were appointed as temastianes (catechists) who conducted the mandatory lessons in doctrine and certain prayer services.

The pre-mission phase was a conscious attempt to create among the Indians strong desires *to invite* the permanent establishment of a mission center. The methods employed during this phase were designed as, or were by nature, means to attract the Indians to cooperative activities ultimately controlled by the Spaniards. Spiritual and political relationships were made; material benefits of contact were offered. The goal was not simply an acceptance of the Spanish presence; it was an enticement to invitation, a kind of social seduction.

Once an Indian group made it sufficiently clear they would accept and support a missionary, the religious superior, or a junta of neighboring priests, would appoint a priest for the inviting tribe. Thus the mission passed into the conversion phase. An invitation was acceptable only after the religious and civil authorities had approved the foundation of a mission because this committed funds from the Patronato Real to the mission as long as it remained occupied. If the priest assigned did not know the language, he spent several months with experienced missionaries who did, or he was furnished with an interpreter who knew the language well enough to assist the Father in liturgical and temporal affairs.

As Pérez de Ribas and Kino pointed out, the Father began his work of conversion by focusing all attention on the church in the village. His entry to take possession of the mission was accompanied by much ceremony, but

---

[42] Frequent reference to imagery and statuary occurs throughout mission literature; cf. Pérez de Ribas, Kino, Nentwig, Pfefferkorn, *passim*. An especially informative critique on their use can be found in the *Informe de la misión de San José de Mátape*, 1744, by Father David Borio; Mateu Collection, Barcelona.

he never delayed or made detours. He went directly to the mission complex already prepared for his arrival. A formal entry was unmistakably stylized. The singleness of direction denoted the singleness of purpose, that is, that the Father had come for the express purpose of making the mission and religion the central organizing activity of the new pueblo.[43]

The organization of common lands, the selection of certain fields for the support of the church, and the division of labor among the able-bodied were matters the missionary worked out in time with the Indians themselves. His first efforts concentrated on using religious ceremony and instruction as vehicles for discipline in the new social organization of the pueblo. Children were gathered together at the ramada or church twice daily. Adults were required to attend on specified days during the week, and then only in the morning.[44] To achieve this much organization the Father depended on the cooperation of native leaders, which created new responsibilities for the neophytes and placed the priest in a time-absorbing role at the ceremonial focal point of village activity.

The priest rose early in the morning to conduct Mass, teach or assist at the teaching of the doctrine in the morning and afternoon, and to conduct evening services before the closing of the church. If there is a preponderance of concern in mission methodology for spiritual affairs, it simply reflects the way in which time was spent in the missions. In temporal, that is, material, affairs the missionary seldom became directly involved, preferring to let the Indians arrive at their own solutions. The Father, of course, acted as final judge to resolve differences of opinion or approach; his remaining apart helped him to preserve a role of judge and arbiter.

The same technique was utilized in punishment and discipline. Missionaries did not mete out the lashes; this was reserved to a minor official in the pueblo. Often the punishment exacted was specified by village law or custom. The missionary permitted the proceedings to arrive at the very moment when an offender was to be whipped; then the Father would step in, releasing the prisoner with a staunch admonition. Such procedures colored the role of the priest with leniency and mercy, thus moderating Spanish authority with some relief and appeal. Force was undeniably used by the missionaries, but it was subject to moderation and a climate of forgiveness to avoid cause for vengeance. Vengeance itself was one of the major obstacles in the Christianization of the natives because it was equated with a rudimentary form of justice in the primitive culture. There are several cases of excessive punishment scattered throughout mission history, but the sum total of all these cases still constitutes only exceptions to the overall manifestation of leniency and rational discipline.

After the mission achieved a relatively permanent acceptance from the Indian tribe, the routine work of evangelization began. The mission now entered on the doctrinal, or pre-parochial, phase of its development. The major concern of the missionary at this time was to instill doctrinal integrity

---

[43] Cf. Pérez de Ribas, *Libro Séptimo*, f. 136.
[44] Cf. Part Two of this text, p. 68, rule 11.

in his flock. Hardly any mission ever accomplished the total numerical conversion of any tribe, but once a mission was firmly established, the task of converting the non-believer diminished as social and political pressures increased on the pagan hold-outs. The missionary's personal conduct remained crucial to the process of persuasion because the Indian converts maintained intimate contact with those who refused to accept baptism.[45]

The missionary's more immediate work dealt with the expansion and correction of the doctrinal content of his people's knowledge. Education was the biggest job. The brighter and more talented children, as well as those of the tribal leaders, were sent off to regional seminaries where they learned to read, write, sing, and play musical instruments.[46] Not all the children could go, nor were all of them permitted to go. Hence, the job of the missionary included the direction of educating the children who stayed behind.

Although the children were taught Spanish and many of the lessons in reading, writing, and basic arithmetic were learned in Spanish usually only the missionary and a handful of trained Indians from another tribe or district actually conducted the lessons. Few, if any, *gente de razón* (educated class) entered the mission compound to assist in teaching because they were not legally permitted such entry — nor did they know the Indian languages sufficiently to be able to teach. The doctrina, or catechism, was taught in both languages with the dual purpose of assuring that the Indians grasped the meaning of the doctrines in their own tongue while providing at the same time a knowledge of Spanish equivalents for some basic ideas. The children learned the bilingual doctrine more readily. The adults often studied the doctrine in their native language under the tutelage of their children who were exposed to the finer nuances by the Spanish-speaking clergy.[47]

As far as it is known, there were no particular or recommended sequences in teaching the catechism. Theoretical and moral concepts were introduced at the discretion of the priest. The content, however, of the catechetical guides was closely regulated by the decrees of the Council of Trent and the subsequent national councils. For example, the Third Mexican Council of 1585 brought Mexico's ecclesiastical laws into conformity with the conciliar decrees, but the Conciliar Commission in Rome, in turn, toned down the stringency of the Mexican bishops. The catechism of the Third Mexican Council was compiled by Father Juan de la Plaza, a former Jesuit Provincial; it probably served as a guide for Jesuit missionaries in the field. But the catechism of Father Jerónimo Ripalda became the more commonly used manual of instruction.[48]

Regardless of the edition in use, the object of catechetical lessons was to insure that the Indian knew the rudiments of Christian belief and devotional practice. The doctrine began with patterned responses to the common

[45] Polzer-Burrus, *Kino's Biography*, p. 199.
[46] Pérez de Ribas, *Libro Séptimo*, f. 136 and 139v.
[47] Cf. AGN. *Jesuitas, Fichero* 2; no *expediente*. Loose pages contain reference to language methods used in doctrina and songs.
[48] ABZ, Vol. I, p. 335. Cf. also E. J. Burrus, "The Third Mexican Council in the Light of the Vatican Archives," *The Americas*, Vol. XXIII (April, 1967), No. 4, pp. 390-407.

prayers used in the Church, that is, the Our Father, Hail Mary, Creed, and the Salve Regina. After an analysis of these prayers, the catechism epitomized the tenets of Christian practice, such as the observance of the command-ments of the Law of God and the Church. The subject matter then passed on to the finer aspects of Christian faith as seen in the role of the sacraments, the works of mercy, the theological and cardinal virtues, the gifts of the Holy Spirit, the Beatitudes and the last things.

According to educational technique, the catechism was based on group response. Significantly, the stress on prayer served both devotional and instructional purposes. In the edition by Father Ignacio Paredes, consulted during the course of this study, there appears a "Doctrina Pequeña" composed by Father Bartolomé Castaño, a former Sonoran missionary.[49] In all prob-ability this shorter and simpler form is typical of the doctrina as taught to the less literate Indians of the north. But there is very little difference in the sequence or content of ideas presented in its "declaraciones."[50] One interest-ing sidelight is the device the catechism uses to teach familial structure and authority in the section on confessional responses:

Penitent. "I talked back once to my father."
  ”   "I talked back in anger twice to my mother."
  ”   "I talked back crossly three times to my grandmother."
  ”   "I talked back four times to my grandmother and
  ”   gave her a bad look."
  ”   "I swore five times at my son with passion and anger."[51]

Not only does the simple pattern provide the nomenclature of social organi-zation, it also antedates by centuries the contemporary language training method of pattern practices.[52]

This developmental stage of the mission experience has been called "pre-parochial" because the objective of the missionary was the completion of the work of conversion by exercising the neophytes in doctrine and devo-tion. Theoretically, the missionary's work extended only to such time as the converted Indian tribes could establish parishes similar to those of the Spaniards. Full conversion was supposed to provide the stability for ecclesi-astical taxation by tithing. In this way the secular clergy could take over the mission-doctrina and have a source of income and support.[53]

---

[49] Castaño was born in Santarén, Portugal, in 1603. He worked in the Sonora missions from 1632 to 1648. He transferred to Oaxaca where he served as rector of the college from 1650 to 1659. He died in Mexico in 1672.

[50] Cf. Gerónimo de Ripalda, *Catecismo Mexicano*, edited by Ignacio de Paredes (México, 1758); copy consulted in Cuevas Collection, Mexico.

[51] Ibid., p. 173.

[52] Cf. *Modern Spanish: A Project of the Modern Language Association.*

[53] Mission funds were paid directly by the Patronato to the orders in charge of the missions. Secular funds came from benefices specified by the Bishop. For a comparison of distribution see Bishop Don Pedro Tapís to the King (Philip V), AGI, *Guad.*, 67-5-15 (cited in Pastells, Vol. XXIII, pp. 513sq.). In explaining the system Tapís noted that no one had been paid from the benefices for twenty years because no secular priests wanted to serve in the frontier reales or pueblos.

No other phase in mission development is more difficult to recognize and describe than the pre-parochial. It is precisely in the evaluation of this stage that the thorny problem of secularization arose. Missionaries insisted the Indians were still learning the rudiments of the Faith; the Bishops insisted they had attained sufficient levels of knowledge and sulf-support to become parishes. And the disputes raged for decades, proving that adequate norms for determining the extent of change were nonexistent.[54]

For the sake of completeness in classifying the stages of mission development, a last phase can be called the "parochial phase." In this stage the emphasis shifted from the refinement of doctrinal instruction to the resolution of the circumstantial problems of acculturation. In other words, many missions reached the point at which the religious preparation was adequate for transfer to secular control, but the lack of sufficient numbers of secular priests to assume parochial responsibilities, the inadequacy of handling native languages, the economic insecurity of the native community, or the instability of political control prevented the transfer to episcopal authority. Some missions were entangled in one or more of these problems for generations. Because of the full parochial involvement in the missions, the Bishops complained that the missions should have been secularized.[55] The Orders retorted that the Indians were not adequately prepared to compete with Spanish society.[56]

What is demonstrated in this final phase is the over-arching character of the mission as an institution of *cultural* change — a function that even the missionaries were slow to realize. When piety provides the presupposition that God's grace, through faith, changes culture (that is, provides something beyond motives), a corollary often results that presupposes the culture of the believer is *the* culture of a Christian. In other words, by identifying faith and culture it is difficult, if not impossible, to accept cultural variants and differences. The Church through its missions arrived at an impasse in presupposing that orthodoxy shaped not only "one faith and one baptism," but one culture as well. By recognizing this impasse the Church should have come to a moment of serious soul-searching about the purpose of missions and the methods of cultural adaptation, but apparently the presuppositions of the era of expansion were too deeply embedded to be questioned.

The missions that reached the parochial phase of development were more exposed than any others to the charge of paternalism. With the primary work of evangelization and conversion complete, the mission system continued with a program of protection for the Indian communities. The secondary purposes of preparing Indians for full participation in Spanish society were much slower of accomplishment. Some historians have shown a tendency to criticize the missions on this basis because once the missionaries were removed by secularization, expulsion, or political collapse, the Indian communities reverted to earlier forms of social organization or were

[54] See Charles Polzer, S.J., "The Evolution of the Jesuit Mission System in Northwestern New Spain, 1600–1767," Ph.D. dissertation, University of Arizona, 1972, Chap. 6.

[55] Cf. AHH, *Temp.* 2009, 2019 and AGN, *Jesuitas* I, exp. 27-28.

[56] Cf. *Tanto Simple*, AHH, *Temp.* 282, exp. 1.

nearly exterminated by exploitation.[57] The resultant disintegration of such native groups seems to prove conclusively that the reasons offered by the missionaries for maintaining protective measures were valid.

If the purposes of the mission program were to retard Indian cultural adaptation, then the charge of paternalism might well be made. But the fact that Indians were not wholly acculturated after many years in a mission does not prove paternalism. The evidence of history indicates that the Spanish social system was probably incapable of preparing and accepting Indians into the more advanced forms of frontier society. In established societies class consciousness was almost rigid.[58] Moreover, Spanish law demanded that those who were entrusted with the care of Indian pueblos carefully protect the community until it could assume full responsibility with the hope of survival.[59]

Probably too much has been made of the interpretation that under Spanish law a mission was to dissolve after ten years. The practice was so universally to the contrary that it is reasonable to conclude that the missions were expected to maintain control until, in the judgment of authorities, independence could safely be granted. To add to the confusion about paternalism, curious misunderstandings about religious poverty and obedience in some historians have not helped to assess the missionary role in the marketplace or in political organization.[60]

Because no manuals of methodology have come to light, the methods used in the missions have been a subject of recurrent speculation. Perhaps the most thorough anthropological study of acculturation in northwest New Spain, Edward Spicer's *Cycles of Conquest*, explored the difference in degrees of acculturation that resulted among Indian groups exposed to Jesuit and Franciscan evangelization. Spicer drew the conclusion that differences in methodology were ultimately responsible for the differences in degree of acculturation.[61] These conclusions, which resulted from the careful application of anthropological method to the ethnological data gathered about these Indian groups, left a serious problem for the historian. There was no historical evidence to substantiate a difference in method between the two religious orders operating in northern New Spain. However, one commentary has now been found and that document substantiates the anthropological speculations of Spicer. This document is a report by a contemporary investigator in 1715, Don Pedro Tapís, Bishop of Durango.[62] Although the document

[57] For example see Hubert Clinton Herring, *History of Latin America from Beginnings to the Present,* p. 188: "The mission village was paternalism flavored with theocracy, a benevolent communalism for the glory of God and the salvation of souls." Also, Bailey Wallys Diffie, *Latin American Civilization: Colonial Period,* p. 583 and pp. 722-726; and Helen Miller Bailey, and Abraham P. Nasatir, *Latin America: The Development of Its Civilization,* p. 182.

[58] Cf. Antonio de and Jorge Juan Ulloa, *Voyage to South America,* 1:29-32.

[59] *Recopilación,* Libro IV.

[60] Cf. Diffie, *Latin American Civilization,* especially pp. 583, 722 and 726.

[61] Cf. Edward H. Spicer, *Cycles of Conquest: The Impact of Spain, Mexico, and the United States on the Indians of the Southwest, 1533–1960,* passim, Chapter 11.

[62] Don Pedro Tapís, Bishop of Durango, to Felipe V. Santa Rosa de Cusiguriachic, Chihuahua, August 26, 1715. AGI, *Guad.,* 67-5-15 (Pastells, Vol. XXIII, p. 503sq.).

is nearly unique in mission literature for comparing methodology between the orders, the findings are significant because they were made by an interested, critical observer who had reason to desire complete success on the part of both religious orders. Tapís' report to the King depends on a single journey of familiarization with his diocese, but he reported cumulative effects that made his observations pertinent to a longer period of time than that of his visitation.

In February, 1715, Don Pedro Tapís, the newly consecrated Bishop of Durango, set out on a visitation of his diocese. Writing the King from the Real of Santa Rosa de Cusiguriachic on August 26, the trail-weary bishop recounted the differences he had witnessed during his journey of nine hundred miles through the missions of the north. At Santa Rosa he had reached the northernmost point in his trip, but nearly two-thirds of his visitation still lay before him. He had travelled through the "most harsh mountains that were almost impassable," but he had seen mission pueblos that rivalled the cathedral of Durango.[63] The entire northern sector of his diocese was plains and deserts far removed from Mexico City and Veracruz; consequently, they lacked trade and communication, which added to his wonderment.

Tapís visited mission-doctrinas under the care of the Franciscans and Jesuits, as well as the reales of the Spaniards where he preached to the people; he omitted preaching in the missions because he did not know the Indian languages. Altogether he visited eleven Jesuit missions by the time he reached Santa Rosa. He had found "the Indians of excellent training and education in both spiritual and temporal matters, as could be seen in the quality and decency of their churches and liturgical worship."[64] Consoled and edified by his visitation of the Jesuit missions, the Bishop of Durango observed that the Fathers of the Society insisted that the Indians learn to read, write, count, and perform other duties.

Much of the customary drinking and dancing had been eradicated which the Bishop considered among the greater abuses of the pagan nations. All in all he found nothing in which to correct the Jesuits. Rather, he was amazed to find in such desolate areas that the missions were well provided, even if in a humble and ordinary way. The Fathers were directing the planting of wheat, corn, and vegetables; cattle raising was a major source of income. Surplus produce was offered for sale and the proceeds were used for building and furnishing churches — a fact which the Bishop testified to as "an eye witness."[65]

While the Bishop was making the visitation of the mission of San Francisco Xavier de Satebó, the pueblo celebrated the feast of St. Ignatius, July 31. The completeness of ceremonies deeply impressed the Bishop because he never suspected the Indians were so well trained and advanced that they could sing a Pontifical Mass to the accompaniment of a bassoon, violin, clarinet, harp, and organ.

---

[63] Ibid.
[64] Ibid., p. 504.
[65] Ibid.

The Indians of the Jesuit missions were well trained and the communities worked cooperatively so that the more needy missions, and even poorer Spaniards, could draw on the more opulent missions for support. The Bishop of Durango reminded the King that the common story held that the missions were too well off and not in need of royal support. But the Bishop had personally witnessed that the Jesuit missions were vigorous centers of growth and Christian charity; he expressed the wish that all the missions and doctrinas would be under the care of the Fathers of the Society because that would be to everyone's consolation and relief.

During the same journey Tapís had visited twelve Franciscan missions. "Everything is so much to the contrary," he reported. Generally the churches operated by the Franciscans were very run down, poorly adorned, and lacked furnishings. The Indians of their missions were poor and went about naked with little instruction or education. The Blessed Sacrament was not kept in reserve in their pueblos.[66]

Obviously, the Bishop of Durango was less than pleased with his findings among the Franciscan missions. In assessing the problems, he concluded that the major difficulty was that superiors changed the missionaries at every chapter, or before. Effectively, then, no Franciscan missionary remained in one place more than two or three years.

There may have been justification for changing the missionaries, but the toll was taken from the Indian communities. The friars looked on their assignments as temporary, so they solicited nothing for the repair or adornment of the churches nor did they acquire things required for liturgical worship. From this it followed, in the Bishop's opinion, that the friars paid little love to the Indians and the Indians were not enamored of the friars. From the lack of cooperation and love, failures in obedience to the missionaries developed. The net result was that education, instruction, and training never evolved. The Indians were not taught how to read, write, or participate musically in liturgical functions. Unfortunately, the Indians who did know these things were only in scattered missions, living in destitution and poverty.

The Franciscans, according to Tapís' observations, took little effort to learn the native languages, or even in teaching the Indians Spanish. As a result they were incapable of administering the sacraments of penance, and the Indians were ill prepared to receive confirmation. The practice in these pueblos had been to invite the Jesuits into the missions to hear confessions and administer confirmation when possible.[67]

The descriptive contrast Bishop Tapís made between the two orders operating in his diocese appears to have been one of the strongest criticisms extant in mission literature of the period. Colorful, virulent attacks against one or other of the orders is not uncommon, but a comparison between two of them by a third party is. And fortunately such uniqueness makes the document all the more useful and applicable. The praise Tapís showered on the Jesuits and the blame he placed on the Franciscans was not done to

---

[66] Ibid., p. 506.
[67] Ibid., pp. 506-509

inflate or deflate egos in the orders. He was attempting to assess the missionary effectiveness of the religious in his diocese. And interestingly enough Tapís took a position on methodology similar to those of Pérez de Ribas and Kino; he stressed the importance of personal communication and warm, mutual acceptance.

The Franciscans did not fail, in his estimation, because they had employed a wrong method; their error was in not communicating effectively and showed minimal concern about acceptance because their assignments were too temporary. The Franciscan problem was poor administration and constant frustration for both priests and Indians. Even the annual stipend from the Royal Treasury was sequestered by the provincials so that nothing was disbursed in the development of the scattered missions.[68]

No single feature of the Jesuit mission method was more important than the knowledge of native languages. Proficiency shaped the key to acculturation And no other single skill was demanded of the missionary as much as his knowledge of Indian language.

Jesuits had to distinguish themselves in reading, writing, and preaching in the Mexican language. Unless they publicly demonstrated mastery, they were not admitted to ordination.[69] Every candidate to the priesthood had to satisfy a board of four examiners who answered to the provincial. Throughout the years many complained of the hardships in learning the language, but the highest superiors staunchly defended the language requirements. Several Jesuits became skilled in two, three, and even four native languages.

Although the northern languages differed significantly from the language of the central valleys, the Mexican language was widespread enough to be useful. Many foreign missionaries, who were sent to New Spain, did not have the advantage of learning Mexican during their course of studies. Often they were ordained before arrival, so the language requirement presented no obstacle before orders. However, all the priests had to satisfy a board of examiners regarding language skills before admission to final vows in the Society. There was no escape.[70]

A period of language apprenticeship was not specified, but new arrivals in mission territory seem to have spent six or more months with an experienced missionary. Depending on the demand, a missionary might spend a year as an assistant while a mission territory was opened, or he might enter a region without prior language skill, especially if the tribal language was totally new and unknown.[71]

Inasmuch as a Jesuit mission method can be spoken of, it would be best summarized as a conscious concern for effective communication with native peoples. Language lay at the base of the methodology and upon its skillful use depended the critical activities of education — reading, writing,

---

[68] Ibid., p. 508.
[69] Cf. Part Two of this text, p. 109; also AHH, *Temp.* 321, exps. 65-71.
[70] The triennial catalogs show *Mexica* was widely used during the first century of expansion. Local dialects gain dominance in the eighteenth century.
[71] Cf. Part Two, p. 110.

arithmetic, the arts, and socio-economic organization. Indeed, the structural development of the mission system revolved around the importance of the regional college where the children of disparate Indian tribes were taught these skills as well as Spanish and Christian doctrine. Beyond this concern for effective communication, the Society of Jesus through its superiors and missionaries in the field stressed the importance of a well disciplined character in the person of the individual missionary. With this kind of person in charge, the door was open to varieties of pragmatic decisions that would achieve the goals of the mission program.

Intercommunication between missionaries, participation in the semi-annual juntas, and frequent visitations by regional superiors supported the uniform development of the mission system. As tribal concerns and circumstances changed with the growing presence of the Spanish colonists, the methods of the missionaries adapted accordingly. Mission goals remained primary, that is, the growth in religious spirit and practice, corporate endeavors to provide for economic security, and growth in literate skills that enabled the Indian to compete with the Spaniard.

The mission community was destined to some degree of failure, not because of the methods employed, but because the rigid social system of colonial Spain made it ultimately impossible for Indian society to rise above the vassalage demanded by the King. The unreality of the mission system was woven into the fabric of Spanish colonial society by unresolved ideals in their concept of Christian humanism. The missions were destined to evolve into a complex system that was irreconcilable with the domineering and expanding colonial society. As the passage of time has shown, the missions were preparing the indigenous populations for nonexistent places in a society dominated by aristocracy and elitism. By the close of the "Jesuit epoch," the mission system was beset by atrophy and plagued by the unresolved problems of secularization.

Part II

Rules and Precepts for the Mission Rectorate of San Francisco Borja, Sonora, Mexico

Translation of Documents
in the Roman Archives of the Society of Jesus

Explanatory material appearing in the original documents
appears herein in parentheses. The author's explanations
are in brackets and in footnotes.

The bells of San Francisco Borja de Tecoripa remind the visitor that this humble place was the headquarters of the rectorate where these Rules and Precepts were recorded.

Rules for the Government
of the Missions As Approved
by the Father Visitor
Rodrigo de Cabredo,[1] 1610

1. INASMUCH as it might be possible on these missions, Ours[2] will accompany one another two by two, one being subordinate to the other, and helping each other through fraternal charity and love in Christ in an enterprise so holy as the assistance of these souls; this will be done in the way in which he who has the charge and care of the district [*partido*] will order. In case they cannot accompany one another, due to a lack of ministers, then at least those two who have neighboring districts and are closest shall arrange to see one another at times to counsel and comfort each other and to communicate the affairs of their souls in this holy society.

2. So that the proper government of these evangelical enterprises, which are so much to the glory of God our Lord and for the salvation of souls, will produce prosperous results and so that these results will certainly fall under the direction of Holy Obedience, Ours are charged that, even though their Superior or Rector is not present, they will have recourse to him in everything so that he can order by his permission those things that are of greater importance in their districts and pueblos. This would apply to entradas for the teaching of doctrine to new pagan tribes who are going to be led to our Holy Faith; this is something that they should not do without first informing their Superior, advising him about the disposition of such tribes to receive the Gospel. In this way all can be performed with the consent of the Superior and his consultors. It will be the same in regard to a church or house that is to be built in some pueblo when that construction will be expensive. Whenever a *reducción* has to be undertaken to improve indoctrination,[3] i.e. when Indians must be physically moved and brought into pueblos, it is fitting that this be done with utmost ease and the least violence possible. The Indians are first to be invited with prayer and kindness, especially those to whose pueblo the others will be joined; agreement about the division of the lands in their district [*distrito*] will be reached with them.

---

[1] Rodrigo de Cabredo, S.J. born 1559 in Navarre, entered the Society of Jesus in 1577, came to Mexico as Visitor General of the Assistancy of New Spain from 1609–1611, and served as Provincial of New Spain from 1611–16.

[2] "Ours" commonly occurs in Jesuit documents and refers to those who belong to the Society of Jesus.

[3] *Reducción* signifies the "leading back" of peoples from uncivilized, rustic living conditions to more highly organized communities as a mission. See page 6.

3. If in any case it becomes necessary for Ours to exercise their spiritual jurisdiction in the external forum[4] in regions that are quite far removed from the Bishops (for which reason their Excellencies have been wont to remit such jurisdiction to religious superiors on the mission), Ours shall take care to exercise their office with the least taint of reproach possible and in a way that it can be understood that the public act was done under the pressure of their office and with edification. It will be the same when punishment is to be meted out to some Indians; it is well known that such cases arise in which punishment is requested, but the Holy Canons do not permit it.[5] Such punishment will be executed by those who govern the people, i.e. by the fiscal of the church or his ministers. Let care be taken that the Indian be aware of his fault.

4. Where there happen to be Reales de Minas, inhabited by neighboring Spaniards, in the lands of those tribes to whom we minister — as the case is today — or whether there be some Presidios of soldiers, both reales and the presidios should have their private pastors or curates. Ours could assist them in their ministry, but this can only be with such attention that no omission will result in their own proper churches or pueblos whose care is primary. They shall advise the Superior of the mission so he can provide a minister during that time when the assigned minister will be absent.

5. Regarding the Spaniards who pertain to Our *doctrinas*[6] because they reside at haciendas or on farms or simply because of the nearness of their habitations, and also regarding the escort soldiers who accompany Ours during dangerous times, these persons will be looked after with all charity and kindness both spiritually and temporally inasmuch as it is possible without interfering with the care of the natives. On the other hand, the escort soldiers are to help and defend against the disturbances that the Indians and the devil by means of his cohorts are wont to raise up. They are to help rid us of disturbances in the preaching of the Gospel and to open the road for the sowing of the seed of the Divine Word.

6. Inasmuch as the mission districts [*partidos*] have smaller divisions [*repartidos*] which in turn consist of various pueblos in their charge, the Fathers will go on a continual visit of them, remaining a suitable number of days in each place so that all may enjoy the bread of the Divine Word and the other ministries. They will leave everything clearly set down for the *fiscales* of the church and for the *temachtianos*, or *maestros*, of doctrine who are the ones who help the people, particularly the children, to learn it. The fiscales should be very punctual in advising the Fathers of those who are ill so that a Father can come to help them and administer the holy sacraments. For those cases in which the Father is by chance absent each pueblo will

---

[4] The external forum refers to the acts of public nature; it contrasts the internal forum or acts that are strictly of private conscience.

[5] An exact reference here would be misleading. Either by extension or interpretation of Canon Law or by proscription in the rules of religious institutes, religious were not permitted to inflict physical punishment. Actual physical punishment was dealt out by a person other than the religious.

[6] Doctrinas are established missions during the teaching or catechetical stage. See page 5 sq.

have an industrious person who knows the form of Baptism so he may baptize those children whose lives are in danger; afterwards he will notify the Father so he can review the action which is so important in the salvation of a soul.

7. Among those Christians more advanced in the faith, although recently converted, the missionary Fathers will take care to introduce the reception of Holy Communion at various times. The Fathers will prepare them for this by explaining this most profound mystery in personal talks; in time they will see that the Indians' capacity for such a divine and important sacrament can be increased. Most especially the Fathers must see that the sick are not deprived of Holy Viaticum which is of such great importance at their moment of need.

8. In accord with what has been said and for the consolation and devotion of the pueblos, and even more for the greater devotion of the Fathers minister of the *doctrina*, let care be taken to place tabernacles in those pueblos where there is an ample church and where Christianity has been better established so that the Most Holy Sacrament may be decently conserved during the days and on the occasions when the priest is present in the pueblo.

9. In the principal pueblo of the district [*partido*] great concern shall be shown for the seminaries of the Indian children where they may be raised in Christian doctrine and virtue. They shall learn to read, write and sing so they can serve in the church and give a wholly virtuous example to the rest of the pueblos. This means has been found to be highly successful in establishing Christianity and in preserving peace in these missions. These seminaries are to be maintained as fittingly as possible, especially in those pueblos where the alms of the King our Lord is so assigned.

10. When a Father has recently come to any of these missions, he shall take care to learn the language proper to the tribe to whom he is assigned. To achieve this he should remain several months in the company of another Father who already knows the language. In case the language is completely new, as sometimes happens, he should be helped by some of the more hispanicized Indians [*más ladino*]. He shall reduce to rules whatever he notes down until he can finally make a grammar of the language so that whoever follows him later can learn the language.

11. When the Superior arrives on his visitation of the district which each of the Fathers has in his charge, which visitation must be once a year, he will be given both a spiritual and temporal account of the state of the district. This will involve whatever touches the greater advancement proper to those of our fellow men whom we have in our charge; as our Father Saint Ignatius teaches we shall desire in everything to be guided by our Superiors who govern us in the place of Christ our Lord. When a missionary is forced on some occasion to become involved with those who have political and temporal control of these people such as the Governor of the Province or the Señor Viceroy who are ordinarily far removed from them and he judges it necessary to appeal or notify them for some remedy, he will not do so without the consultation and approval of the Mission Superior nor without notifying the Father Provincial of Mexico so that he can deal with his Excellency or the

Father whom he will have appointed in his place. This is necessary if a suitable remedy is to be found in matters of such importance as peace or the *reducción* of new peoples to our holy Faith. And moreover, it is necessary if the least offense possible is to be avoided to all parties concerned.

12. Ours ought to encourage and introduce the Indians to beneficial works which will eradicate the laziness that is the root and mother of all vices; in this way they can live a more politically organized life thus earning enough to clothe and maintain themselves. But this must be done first with gentleness and never with harshness so that they will not lose hope and other pagan tribes will not get the impression that Christian living is merely for working or a form of captivity. For the same reasons Ours on no occasion will ever assess the Indians of their districts with labor in the haciendas of Spanish neighbors. Whether Indians are to be hired or not is to be left to their judgment. Where there might be *repartidor*-judges [i.e., labor referees] appointed to govern them, the missionaries will counsel them to exercise their office toward the Indians with the least offense possible. Experience teaches that the natives who apply themselves more readily to work are less prone to uprisings and disturbances among themselves.

13. Whenever the Indians or the Spaniards who are in some of our districts [*distritos*] offer stipends for determined days or on other occasions during the year, let them be applied to the Church and to those who serve in it so that the Institute and rules of the Society may be observed with greater purity because we have always professed that no stipend shall be levied for our ministries.

14. The Fathers who are attached to each of the mission cabeceras under separate governance will meet with their Superior twice annually at a suitable place where all may assist without going a long way from their districts. Thus gathered together for a period of at least eight days, they will keep a common order with full observance of the distribution of religious exercises as is done in the colleges of the Society. During this time the fathers will discuss and treat of the means by which they can better promote Christianity among these peoples; let them deliberate about the things that have been attempted or could be tried in these conversions because very frequently the Doctors are neither specific nor practical in these matters. Moreover, there shall be a conference given to the community by a Father designated by the Superior; the conference will deal with religious observance and perfection, and the zeal for them; this will be applied to the exercise of our ministries which seek holiness in living. At this time the Fathers should disclose their temporal needs, e.g. clothing, Mass wine, medicines for the sick, etc. so that in lands so remote and poor the alms which the King our Lord has designated in the Royal Treasury of Mexico can be used to fill these needs. Because we profess religious poverty, these *memorias* will be remitted to the procurator general of Mexico duly signed by the Superior so that all will come with the blessing of obedience.

15. If anyone of the Fathers, because of a prevailing illness in his district or because some other accident may have happened, is not able to meet with the rest of the Fathers at one of the two juntas held each year, he will

make certain not to miss the following one so that it will never happen that he is not present at least once a year. Because each one of the Fathers is obligated to make the Exercises of Saint Ignatius for eight days according to the rule which we have in the Society, he will be absent from his mission during that period while he makes those exercises which are held ordinarily at the house of the mission cabecera where the Superior customarily assists; the missionary will leave his district in charge of the Father who is his neighbor, taking care to inform him if anyone is ill so that he can comfort him with the holy sacraments lest there be a failure in fulfilling such an exact obligation.

16. These special regulations, over and above the common rules of the Order which are to be carried very much before the eyes of our apostolic and religious ministers, will govern Ours in such a way that although they live outside our communities and colleges they will be governed as if in them since it is holy obedience that places them in these works, enterprises and missions which are so much to the glory of God and proper to the apostolic Institute of our Society. All the aforementioned means, by which religious perfection is preserved, will aid in the salvation of souls without disturbing the attainment of the two purposes for which God instituted and called this Society as soldiers in his militia. These soldiers will wander through these missions as long as holy obedience holds them there; they cannot be changed without an order from Father Provincial who will be notified when by reason of poor health or lack of strength for the labors of these missions it might seem best to grant permission to return. Then his Reverence will substitute others to take his place; the Provincial may do the same when others who have worked on the missions for several years desire to return, being consoled by the companionship of their brothers in the colleges and in our houses.

The Regulations
Made by the Visitors General
for the Whole Province, and by the Provincials
for the Missions, 1662

(These are the common rules for all the missionary fathers which were made by Father Hernando de Cabrero, Visitor of this Province, at the first *junta*, which was held in the College of Guadalajara, March 25, 1662, and at the second *junta*, which was held in the College of Santa Ana on April 20 of the same year. For the good government of these missions the missionary fathers of Sinaloa, Sonora, the Sierra, the Tarahumaras and the Tepeguanes made a resume of all the regulations they had. They conferred again with other missionaries, Father Provincial Pedro Antonio Díaz, and the Province consultors on September 20, 1662. Because these missionaries presented me with the great difficulty they have in practicing some of these rules and because some rules are no longer applicable, because so many years have gone by and circumstances have changed, it seemed necessary to make a new compendium which could be more easily read and placed in execution.)

1. It is presumed that the principal purpose of these missions is to attend to the spiritual welfare of the Indians because of the great need they have in being helped. After the exact observance of the rules and the punctuality which ought to be had in performing spiritual exercises, which is the first thing that the missionaries ought to attend to, the following things are ordered:

2. Primarily it is ordered that no one will go alone to hear confessions, to exercise other ministries, or to do anything else. Everyone will conform to what has been set down in Instructions 3 and 15 for Confessors.[7] When missionaries, by reason of their isolation or great distances, cannot accompany one another, every precaution will be taken on what touches decency and security; the missionaries will always go with the fiscal or some other Indian who can better supply for the lack of a companion.

3. When any missionary leaves his district for another, whether it be from the Sierra or from Sinaloa or Sonora, or from the Tepehuanes and the Tarahumares, the Father Visitor of the said mission will assign for him the number of pack animals he can take. This number shall conform to the distance to be travelled. However, if the missionary must leave the province, then the following order will be kept: a) if he departs from the Sierra, he will take 6 or 8 mules; the same will be taken by the Fathers of the Tepehuan

---

[7] The Rules for Confessors: The Society issued special rules for priests, missionaries, provincials, etc. The specific ruling mentioned here is uncertain because the numbering and wording of the rules has occasionally changed. This reference, however, is most probably to the use of screens between the penitent and confessor.

and Tarahumara missions; b) if he departs from Sinaloa he will take 10 pack animals; c) if he departs from Sonora, he will take 12 because all will be needed since many will die on such a long journey; d) let him give an account to his immediate superior and to the Visitor of the mission as well as to the procurator of the province of all he has taken. Whatever surplus or whatever number of mules remain will be reported so that restitution can be made to the district from which they came; e) whatever the King has given in alms to the missions, and especially whatever may have been given any missionary who has died, shall be remitted to the district where he worked and died; f) when someone leaves the missions for a house or college, or goes from one district to another, he will not take with him the ornaments of the house or church, or anything else whatsoever from the district where he was staying. He may, however, purchase them with his alms. With permission he is only allowed to take a *Bible, Summa,* and a *Contempt of the World* (A'Kempis) or a book of devotion. If he should take anything else, it will be only with the permission of his immediate superior who will have notified the Father Visitor.

4. All missionaries who leave or change their districts or who return to the Province shall leave signed *memorias* and inventories of the furnishings of the house and church. The Father Visitor will review and countersign them when he makes his visitation; the newly arrived Father will also sign them. Let this Father attend to what he does and what he signs so that he will not have to account for something lacking and so that something additional will not have to be added afterwards.

5. All the *memorias* which Ours shall send to the Province Procurator will be sent registered and signed by the immediate superior of the mission where the missionary resides. They will not ask for anything that is superfluous as this is against our religious profession, nor will they ask for things for use of secular persons even though they are relatives. Whatever is seriously entrusted to the superiors, which also applies if any money is sent to Mexico to pay for the items ordered in the memoria, must be registered and signed by the immediate superior of the mission; he will see to it that the order is modest as it ought to be. Only that will be expedited which can absolutely be bought and paid for with the alms provided; the rest will be bought conditionally in case there are price increases. If any missionary finds himself in need of more assistance for his personal sustenance, clothing, or travel, he may not sell the furnishings of the house and much less of the church. In such instances he will have recourse to the superior who will see how his needs can be provided for.

6. Each of the missionaries will have an account book in which he will record all that he has received, whether that be clothing, money, or anything else; and separately he will keep an account of all expenditures. At the time of the juntas the superior will balance the accounts, and later the Visitor will do the same during his visitation. Moreover, in each district there will be a book in which all the furnishings that belong to the church and the house are recorded; this will serve as the account to be used during the visitation.

7. The accounts which the Province Procurator sends to the missionaries will also pass through the hands of the immediate superior so he can see how the accounts of the subjects are faring with the Procurator so no debts will accumulate.

8. The missionaries will not commission the sowing of fields in order to distribute produce to the Indians by obliging them to work in them. They will so commission only what is necessary for their sustenance. It will suffice for this to give them the necessary direction for their own welfare. The Indians should be persuaded with gentleness but never harassed with tasks and duties in order to make a profit or engage in business because this is strictly forbidden.

9. Let all the missionary Fathers take care to show the Indians all love and charity in their dealings; they ought to avoid as much as possible all forms of strictness and harshness. For this reason let no one have in his house any stocks or shackles to imprison them. If it becomes necessary at any time to punish them, it will be done at the hands of the justices of the pueblo. Should an Indian have to be placed in the stocks at the order of the Father, he will not be placed in them by his head, nor will he be forced to sleep in them. In those regions where flogging has been introduced as a punishment for being absent from the doctrina, or for some similar offense, it will be done only with notable moderation lest the Indians lose their love for their pastors.

10. Whenever the Indians are to be brought out of their mountain retreats and rancherías into the pueblos, let this be done with complete gentleness. This shall be done through the ministers of the Lord Governor or through Indians already members of the group; thus we shall completely avoid violence on our part.

11. It is not necessary to oblige the Indians to come to the church or to the doctrina both morning and evening on feast days; it will suffice that they come in the morning. It is not necessary that they come at all on work days unless the Fathers have come to visit their district. While the Fathers are staying in the district, the Indians shall come to the doctrina on the first three or four days, but they need not come every day during their stay; the children, however, will come every day both morning and evening.

12. No one will construct a house or church of any significance without notifying Father Provincial; nor shall anyone modify or move the church. If an urgent case arises which the superior and consultors judge is impossible to get the prior permission of the Provincial, then the Provincial will be notified of everything as soon as possible.

13. The missionaries, even though they are superiors, will not consign any Indians for labor as miners or laborers in *repartimiento* either by themselves or through any intermediary.[8] The Indians are to be left at full liberty to hire themselves out to whomsoever they choose. The Fathers will not impede the work of the *repartidores* or the justices. If any inconvenience should arise wherein this cannot be achieved with good results, let the Fathers advise the Father Visitor so that he can take the matter up with the Captains or with the Lord Governor for a fitting solution.

---

8 *"Repartimiento"* refers to the distribution or allotment of Indian labor.

14. The office of Vicar will not be solicited and none of Ours will be admitted to it, regardless of whether the Lord Bishops ask for it or whether the seat is vacant. In these matters proceed with serious attention and prudence along with the counsel and advice of those Fathers closest to the Bishop. Remit to the Bishop the cases and the matrimonial pleas that can be an occasion of unrest.

15. In each district there is to be a book which records those baptized and their godparents. Those who have been married and who have died are also to be recorded. Ordinarily these will be three books: one of Baptisms, another of marriages, and a third of the deceased.

16. All shall provide for the hiring of soldiers who can go where the missionaries reside because they are the defense against the fights among Indians. If the Fathers have to feed the soldiers because there is no other place where they can seek food, let it be provided that they do not dine with the Fathers. This understanding applies to Sonora and Sinaloa, but in the rest of the mission the Fathers will maintain the customs which they have always followed in order to avoid inconveniences and occasions of displeasure.

17. Inasmuch as possible Ours will avoid writing letters to Ours complaining about the laity. If a letter has to be written, let it be so done that, even if lost or opened, the person about whom the letter was written could not understand it. The same caution is to be observed when writing the Provincial about things that must be dealt with secretly because experience has shown the contrary practice creates grave inconveniences.

18. The juntas of Ours will be held twice annually, on the feast of the Epiphany and afterwards on Corpus Christi, in the region and place which seems best to the immediate superior of the mission. During the days of the junta exact religious discipline will be kept; all will assist at all functions at the sound of the bell as is customary in our colleges. Two or three hours daily will be devoted to conferences on cases of conscience which each one might have, communicating them first to the superior. Another day or days shall be set aside for the reading of the Summary of the Constitutions and the Common Rules, the Rules of Modesty; of Priests; of Preachers; of Missionaries; the general notices, precepts, and censures of the Society; the letter of obedience of Our Holy Father Saint Ignatius; and the other things that have been printed by our Fathers General; and the regulations of the Fathers Visitor and the Provincials. At these two juntas will be held the renovation of vows and the Fathers will give an account of their conscience as is customary in our Society. Unless postponed to the time of the Exercises or the junta which is held at Corpus Christi when each Father has to bring the annual remarks on his district, a general confession shall be made. Regarding the annual remarks, these will be entrusted to the superior so that he can remit copies to Mexico to Father Provincial; the originals will be left at the cabecera of the mission. At each of the juntas the superior has to give an exhortation or a spiritual conference.

19. In no case is an Indian woman, even though she is a little girl, or any woman whosoever to be permitted to enter our houses; all services that are required in the house shall be done by reliable men.

20. All of our missionary priests will make their spiritual exercises once a year in the following way: each Father will see who lives closest to his district and he will go there to make the exercises in the said Father's house for the space of eight days. He will leave only after first hearing the confessions of the sick and arranging things so that nothing is wanting in his pueblo during his absence. If it should happen that he is unable to make them, the superior will inform the Provincial so that he can fulfill what was ordered by the Eighth General Congregation, Decree 38.[9]

21. All of Ours will be careful in their communications with the laity especially in disclosing to them unfitting matters or what may concern the reputation of another, or disagreements among Ours, or what may redound to someone's discredit.

22. Every kind of profit-making, business with the laity, sales or bartering of items is prohibited. The prohibition is such that immediate superiors cannot give permission for this. The only permissible sale is of surplus for the ornamentation and furnishing of the church which is to be done under the supervision of the superior. Inasmuch as the needs of the missionaries require them to have pack-animals and mounts for their provisions and other needs around the house such as remunerating the fiscales, cantors, and other ministers of the church for their work and to keep them pleased and content, the Fathers Visitor are permitted, with the consultation of the immediate superiors and other Fathers, to designate a place in the missions of their visitation purposely for raising these animals to aid the missionaries. Let them use a discrete and well-ordered charity in judging what is necessary so there will be no failure to have in each district the mares required to guard the livestock from which they are ordinarily maintained. In no way will it be permitted, just as it was formerly strictly prohibited, to sell these mounts. The care of this establishment, which will be entrusted to someone judged suitable, and the distribution of what each mission wants will be left to the immediate superiors so they can judge what seems best in the Lord. In order to avoid the problems that are contingent on an oversupply of wheat and corn, it is ordered that no one plant more than the superior judges necessary whether this be for the missionary's house or for the building and furnishing of the church.

23. No Father will employ a Spaniard whether he be a mestizo or mulatto; only Indians from his district will be employed as the minor foremen of flocks or as agents to take the produce to market. Only the Fathers in the Tarahumara mission may employ *gente de razón* who are not Indians; they may care for the house whenever the Father has to be absent because due to the Indians' frequent drunkenness damage might occur.

24. Let the Fathers be scrupulous in absenting themselves from their districts to go to the Spanish *Reales*. They will not beg without permission of the Provincial, nor will they wander about from one pueblo to another. Let them investigate to see if anyone knows how to baptize during their

---

[9] The Eighth General Congregation of the Society of Jesus met in Rome November 21, 1645, through April 14, 1646. Decree 38 commanded each priest to make an eight-day retreat annually. No one was excused, and any person asking to be excused had to submit his reasons to the Provincial only.

absences, and let them rebaptize under condition those apparently baptized.

25. Care will be taken to administer the Holy Oils and Viaticum to whoever needs it. All will make a catalog of their flocks. For Baptism the Fathers will not require that the doctrine be known from memory because of the danger of death or loss of judgment.

26. Indians who wish to marry or to live in another district will not be prevented therefrom by violence. Let the Fathers take notice that they should not induce the Indians into these actions, nor should they easily admit Indians from other districts into their own. Rather, they should persuade them with good reasons to return. If the Indians are admitted into the district, the Father in charge of the former district should be notified so it can be determined if the ones admitted are delinquents or if for some reason they ought to be returned. They should find out whether the Indians are bachelors or married men, and if women are accompanying them, whether they come legitimately or are stolen (which is something they ought to attend to first).

27. Let everyone understand that the superior of each mission can administer the sacraments in each district of the mission since he holds the most primary designation; it is fitting, however, that he not do so without necessity.

28. Although it would be most consoling and edifying if each mission cabecera reserved the most Holy Sacrament, this is prohibited except during the juntas of the Fathers because of the inconstancy of the Indians and the risk involved. Also, no procession shall be held on the feast of Corpus Christi unless other priests, Spaniards, or well established natives attend.

29. Great care shall be taken with the seminaries of children and Indians. Whoever is in charge will teach them doctrine, and how to read, write and sing. When the Father Visitor makes his visitation, he will see how this is done so that nothing will be deficient.

30. New expeditions among pagan peoples will not be undertaken without a prior consultation with the superior of the mission, the Father Visitor, and other Fathers. It will be the duty of the Father Visitor to write the Provincial expressing his opinion and that of those consulted. In every case the Provincial's reply and resolution will be awaited; he will reply as quickly as possible especially if his attention is called to the need.

31. No Father on the missions will write to the Lord Governor of this kingdom or to the Captain of Sinaloa on any business or matter of importance which could result in some bad feeling or other inconvenience without first showing the letter to the superior of the mission. Even though it might seem all right, the opened letter will be sent to the rector at Guadiana or to another superior in the neighborhood of Parral where the Governor or the Captain of Sinaloa assists. If the letter is destined for the Captain of that presidio, he can give it to him or not as seems best. This same regulation will be observed by the superiors of the missions who have to write the Viceroy; these letters will be sent open to the Provincial or whoever is in his place in Mexico. And the same regulation is to be observed when one writes the Audiencia of Guadalajara or to the Señor Bishop; these letters must first go to the Father Visitor.

32. The Superior of a mission may not change or barter anything from

one district to another in any way that fixes it firmly without consulting the Father Visitor and having both Fathers arrive at an agreement with him. If the case is so grave and extraordinary that the advice and consent of the Father Visitor could not be gotten, then the superior will give a complete account to the Provincial at the first opportunity. [The margin notes in another handwriting that this rule needs explanation regarding the goods of residents.]

33. The Fathers will not fail to lock the doors of the church at the Ave Marias;[10] even though there be a crowd awaiting confessions; they will have to return the following morning.

34. Superfluous expenses for food on our feasts will be avoided. On none of our feasts will more than four dishes of meat be provided in addition to the two plates before and the two desserts of fruit. This applies even when externs are present since they never give Ours more than two plates of meat over and above the main serving.

35. Our Fathers are gravely cautioned that no Indian boy or girl is to be sent from their districts to serve any lay person. The Fathers are not to surrender any of the Indian children to any lay person on any pretext or for any reason. Neither superiors nor Visitors can give this permission.

36. No Father can become involved in giving or releasing farm-sites to Spaniards who hold them in equity nor can they hinder other payments which are reasonably held. In the event the Indians are being molested this way, the Fathers will inform their immediate superiors who will, in turn, notify the Father Visitor. When it becomes necessary he will have recourse to the Lord Governor so he can remedy it.

37. None of Ours will send as a present to any lay person any product of the land without permission of the superior because the rules pertaining to the vow of poverty (i.e. that one may neither give nor receive anything without permission) are no less in force on the missions than in the colleges. In the more ordinary cases each one will consult his superior about what can be done.

38. The regulation of Father Visitor Rodrigo de Cabredo, confirmed by various letters of the Fathers General, that no one shall go to the church to talk to or to confess any Indian woman, much less a Spanish one, without the public presence of a person of age shall remain in effect. Also, the confession is only permitted when the 15th Rule of Priests regarding the hearing of confessions is kept.[11] In some places there may be difficulty for the Indians to make their ordinary confessions by counting their sins on little cords, but everything possible must always be done to comply with what the rule demands.

---

[10] The "Ave Marias" are known commonly as the "Angelus." This is the noon and evening prayer by which Christians commemorate the Incarnation, using verses of the Gospel of Luke followed by the brief prayer, the Hail Mary.

[11] The 15th Rule of Priests required that when hearing confessions the priest should avoid any change in facial expression. He was to listen to the penitent freely and attentively. If no confessional was available, the priest was to interpose his hand between himself and the penitent. In no case was a woman's confession to be heard without an intervening screen unless illness or necessity required otherwise.

39. Generally speaking, unity and conformity is commended to our Fathers with one another and with others. This should be without scandal to the Spaniards or the Indians. Furthermore they should attend carefully to the cult and reverence of the churches in the matter of maintaining silence and not permitting the use of chocolate, or anything else to eat or drink, in them.

40. It has been noticed that some of the missionaries who have learned the Indian language have left the missions without writing it down. The missionary successor then has to work twice as hard to learn it for himself. Hence, it is ordered that the Fathers will be careful in this regard so the labors of some will serve the others.

41. Alms are of no further service here; it was happening at times that the Rector of Sinaloa was selling the herd for the alms.

42. From now on the Father Visitor will stipulate during the junta the quantity which each mission can plant according to what seems sufficient to him for the maintenance of each missionary so that there will be no excesses that can occasion murmuring among the laity. The practice of planting corn which has been introduced for the needs of the church will not be abandoned for this reason.

43. The missionary Fathers will not contract debts, even though in small sums, without the permission of the superior because many inconveniences follow from it such as the impediments they present in leaving a pueblo where they have been living when the Fathers are recalled to the Province.

44. As is the custom, baptismal fonts will always be placed in the churches and not in the sacristies.

45. The Fathers who are the proper curates of those who live in their districts, whether Spaniards or Indians, are to remember that one of their obligations is to bury the dead and say Masses for their souls when this is requested out of devotion. So too, they are obligated to the spiritual and temporal needs of those who pass through their districts just as if they were residents of the district when they become ill or die. If the Fathers fulfill their obligations of saying Masses and burying the dead without accepting the customary alms, it would not be possible for them to say Masses which are enjoined by the Constitutions and by order of our Father General; the burden would be too great to be borne. Hence it is declared fitting that for Masses and burials the customary alms may be levied; with this they can say as many other Masses as they have said in fulfilling their obligations. If any surplus accrues, it may be used at the will of the missionaries for something for the church.

46. It is good that the Missionary Fathers know that Indians who are not capable of receiving communion can gain the *jubileo* [indulgence] by merely making their confession; this through a Brief conceded by the Holy See at the instance of the King to the effect that when the confessor judges the Indian should not receive communion, he can still enjoy the indulgence although the indulgence itself would normally require the reception of communion.

47. Two memorias or inventories will be maintained. One will record

what the King has given the Indians for the church in their district; the other, what Ours have given from their alms to the said church so that an account will be available detailing who donated what.

48. Let careful attention be paid to that which pertains to religious modesty. No one will use a cloth cap in his district, not when walking around or on any occasion. Interior clothing will be kept modestly as our state requires. None of Ours will use an arquebus, carbine or other weapon; these are not even to be carried. The Father Visitor is charged with the responsibility of not permitting any similar disorder; he is to admonish and punish offenders if it becomes necessary. Similarly the immediate superiors are obliged to inform the provincial once a year of these observances and they are to notify the Father Visitor of anyone having weapons under the provision that if this cannot be remedied, the superiors will be obliged to command the party under precept.

49. Father Alonso Bonifacio, as Provincial of this Province, hereby sets down this precept under virtue of Holy obedience that each and every and all missionaries will not send outside the Province either by himself or by a third party whether for Ours or for any extern of any station whatsoever, or whether by contract or for profit, friendship, or on a pretext of pious devotion anything which the earth provides or that human industry can produce to the value of even one peso without the explicit permission of Father Visitor.[12] Nor will Ours be able to supply laymen whether they reside in the Province or are coming and going from it; they can only supply those of Ours who are resident in the Province and then only in that which would promote union and charity among one another in conformity with the permission communicated by their superiors for that purpose. In explaining this precept Father Francisco Calderón said: 1) that not even the Father Visitor could give permission for things which involved contracts or profit-making because these actions are not licit. 2) that for sending anything of this kind which might assist the missionaries and which charity among Ours might demand, whether this be within the Province or outside it, it would suffice that the immediate superior give permission. This precept, having been promulgated, was reviewed by Father Provincial Antonio Díaz and his consultors; it seemed to them that it ought to remain in force.[13]

50. Likewise, when Father Alonso Bonifacio was Visitor on these missions, he set down another precept binding all missionaries under obedience; the precept was to be followed literally and not subject to any interpretation. He ordered that Ours were prohibited from making entradas into pagan lands until such time as the Father Provincial had been informed by the Father Visitor and an answer had been returned. The Fathers must wait for the Provincial's reply as noted in regulation 30. It was unanimously agreed

---

[12] Alonso Bonifacio, S.J., born Toledo in 1592, entered the Society in 1608, made his final profession in 1626. He served as Provincial of New Spain from 1634–37 and again from 1641–44; he died at the College of Mexico, December 13, 1667.

[13] Francisco Calderón, S.J., born 1596 in Alcalá, Spain, entered the Society in 1601, professed final vows in 1619. He served as Provincial from 1644–46 and again in 1653 when he resigned after a few months in office. He died in Mexico City, July 13, 1661.

that this precept, having been reviewed by Father Provincial Pedro Antonio Díaz[14] and the Province consultors, will remain in force.

51. Regarding the precept of Father Provincial Andrés de Rada[15] that none of Ours who leave a district for another in that mission or for any other place, nor his successor, can remove anything from the church or house to another district; they shall leave everything just the way it was. It seemed to the Provincial and the consultors that this precept should be rescinded and only the rule left in force. All understood that whatever rule or precept which was made by either the Visitors sent by our Father General or by the Provincials does not expire with their terms of office but remains in force until revoked or superseded.

A copy of these regulations should be available in each district for the missionaries who are there. The regulations should be read frequently and the superior will read them to the Fathers so he can see they are followed. It should also be noted that these are the only rules to remain in force because all the rest which have ever been written by former Visitors and Provincials have been left in this compendium.

Mexico, 20 September 1662

---

[14] Pedro Antonio Díaz, S.J., born 1596 in Cascante, Navarre, entered the Society in 1615, and made his profession in 1632. He was Provincial in 1660 when the Visitor General Hernando Cabredo arrived in 1661. Díaz died around 1670.

[15] Andrés de Rada, S.J., born 1599 in Belmontanes (Cuenca), Spain, entered the Society in 1616, and made his profession in 1637. He was Provincial of New Spain, 1649–1653. In 1662 he acted as Visitor General to Peru; his name drops from mention in the Mexican catalogs after 1671.

Regulations
for the Visitors, 1662

In order to resolve any doubts which may have arisen up to now and to avoid any doubts in the future that may stem from the regulations which the Fathers Provincial have made concerning the jurisdiction of the Fathers Visitor of the missions, the Provincial, Pedro Antonio Díaz, and the Province consultors have reviewed these regulations for some time and it seems fitting to issue the following orders:

1. It is supposed that the Visitors of the missions are assigned by the Provincial in order to supply for his absence in normal visitations and extraordinary or urgent matters. But it is apparently necessary to state that the said Visitors, once they have completed their visitation just as the Father Provincial does in the colleges, will leave the exercise of authority and ordinary jurisdiction to the immediate superiors who will do what they judge best.

2. So that the governing by the Father Visitor may be more certain, the Visitors will have an admonitor and consultors who are to be appointed by the Provincial. These persons may be consulted on important points which will be brought to their attention by the immediate superiors and whatever else may be communicated to them.

3. The Visitor's term of office will last until a successor is appointed by the Provincial. He will perform these duties and during his three year term he will visit the missions and other places in his charge at least twice.

4. The office of Visitor is so called not for a lack of a better name, but because the purpose for which it was instituted is to visit the missions twice during the three year term as has been stated. Let him personally visit the missions in his charge and see his subjects in their own districts where he can take their accounts of conscience, make a report on how each one is doing spiritually as this pertains to religious observance, take an account of the mission's temporal affairs, and observe what kind of example the missionary gives, how he administers the sacraments, how he cares for the furnishing of the churches, and if he treats the Indians with the love of a father. Moreover, he should review the three books of Baptisms, Marriages, and Deaths, the church and house inventories, and the book of income and expense from the alms. The Visitor will advise each one as well as the immediate superior of what is to be done or to be corrected; the execution of this will be left to the respective superior.

5. The second purpose for which the office of Visitor was instituted is that each time a visitation is made, the Visitor will afterwards send a report of everything to Father Provincial, informing him of what has been done and how each particular subject is faring.

6. The third purpose for the Visitor is that when an urgent case arises, or because of some mishap, it is best that someone leave the missions to return to the Province, the Visitor can send him on to one of the colleges at Guadalajara or Guadiana; but the Visitor shall not send him to any other college without the permission of the Provincial. It will be best for the missionaries of Sinaloa and Sonora to go to Guadalajara and those from the Sierra and the Tarahumara to go to Guadiana where they can await the Provincial's reply which will tell them what is to be done.

7. It also pertains to the Visitor's office to deal with the Governors and Captains concerning those things that involve the pacification of Indians or the entradas which seem fitting to undertake.

8. The Visitors are not able to transfer anything from any district from either a church or house without first notifying the Provincial and awaiting his reply. The Visitors cannot designate immediate superiors because this is reserved to the Provincial.

9. If any dispute arises between mission superiors, the Visitors have authority to determine what seems best, most reasonable, and just after having listened to both sides. The superiors have to do what the Visitors resolve, but it would be best if the Visitors first consulted with one or more of their advisors; this same procedure is understood to apply to a difference that arises between subject and superior. Although the Visitors do not have to listen easily to the complaints of subjects about their superiors, nevertheless, the door should not be closed to them and much less so if it is evident they have sufficient cause.

10. The Visitors can change a subject from one district to another, or from one mission to another, if they judge it best for the subject and useful for the Indians. But this is not to be done without grave need and consultation.

11. In the event there is no Visitor because of death or some other cause and some grave matter arises in which delay would be dangerous while the matter is being brought before the Provincial, the Rector of the Villa will act in his place.[16] This will follow the new organization since the Visitor's jurisdiction has been divided; in the place of the Visitor of Sonora such substitution will be made by the Rector of the mission of San Francisco Xavier.

12. While the Visitors are making their visitation, they will not take a companion; rather, the Father of one district can accompany him to another so there will not be a lack of ministers in any one district. In the manner of travel, as in their reception and dealings, the Visitors will avoid those things that are foreign to our way of life. Let them take care to give an example

---

[16] The "Villa" refers to the Villa of San Felipe on the Río Sinaloa. The original Jesuit missionary base was established here and about 1610 it became the location of the Jesuit College of Sinaloa.

Ritual of Feasts

First Vespers	Missa Cantata	Procession
Circumcision	Circumcision Epiphany	Circumcision
Purification	Purification	
		Palm Sunday Holy Week
	Resurrection	Resurrection
Ascension		
Corpus Christi	Corpus Christi	Corpus Christi
St. Ignatius	St. Ignatius	St. Ignatius
Assumption		Assumption
Nativity of BVM	Nativity of BVM	Nativity of BVM
St. Michael	St. Michael St. Louis Gonzaga Holy Apostles St. John Baptist	St. Michael
All Saints	All Saints St. Francisco Borja	
St. Francis Xavier	St. Francis Xavier	
Immaculate Conception	Immaculate Conception	
Christmas	Christmas	
Patron of Pueblo	Patron of Pueblo	Patron of Pueblo
		Mondays: for the dead; with responses, in the cemetery

Masses of Our Lady

Saturdays and Feasts of the Virgin

They will preach every Sunday and on all feasts for the Indians.

of modesty and humility which our rules enjoin and which our first Fathers have shown us.

Although these rules as herein set down provide sufficiently for most instances, I cannot refrain from encouraging immediate superiors, Visitors and Provincials, with all possible insistence, that they show a special interest in the missionary Fathers because this is a most effective means for advancing the missions. They ought to pay particular attention to counsel them, taking care to esteem them, as is only just, and to assist them in whatever way they need. Let them be shown gratitude for their notable works because all this serves to encourage them to apply themselves to their apostolic ministries.

Mexico, 20 September 1662

The Jesuit mission church of San Francisco Xavier del Batuco. Normally inundated by the waters of El Novillo dam, this church once was in the charge of Father Francisco X. Door.

Regulations of
Father Visitor
Juan Ortiz Zapata, 1678

Consequent to the visitation of the Missions made by Father Juan Ortiz Zapata[17] at the order of Father Provincial Tomás Altamirano, and conforming to his orders, the immediate superiors and local visitors on each mission are charged with the following points so they may be executed with holy zeal and care:

1. Father Provincial enjoins with much efficacy that the temporal affairs of our missions be conducted in such a way as to promote the proper spiritual goals such as the care of souls. A great deal of special care should be taken in religious discipline, in the exercises of prayer, examen, spiritual reading, and the account of conscience together with the observance of our Institute and the orders of superiors regarding the good government of our missions.

2. Care is to be taken to provide themselves with wine and hosts from Mexico or elsewhere so that Mass can be celebrated daily in conformity with our rules. They should take particular care of the military in those places where there are no priests so that the faithful will not be deprived of the spiritual benefits of this sacrifice as has been noted as the usual result when a Father does not celebrate each day.

3. The missionaries are not to absent themselves from the juntas which are held twice annually as has been ordered. At the junta they are to observe the established religious order at the sound of the bell. The rules and regulations are to be read together with whatever else the superior shall judge ought to be read from the Institute. Let there be consultations on cases of conscience and let them renew their vows.

4. The Exercises are to be made each year with complete exactness.

5. Concerning the administration of the mission, special care shall be taken of the Indians especially in explaining the doctrine so they can come to understand the mysteries of our Holy Faith which they have to believe and the commandments which they have to keep to be saved. The Indians should receive talks on Sundays, feast days, and other days that seem appropriate. So these goals can be realized the missionaries will take particular care in learning the languages current in the district. The children will assist at doctrine in the morning and afternoon; care will be taken to see that they review it and learn it.

---

[17] Juan Ortiz Zapata, S.J., born in Zacatecas in 1620, entered the Society in 1639, and made his profession in 1656. He spent most of his later years at the College of Saints Peter and Paul in Mexico City, where he died in 1687.

6. Care will be taken in the seminaries so that those who are capable will learn to read and write, and to sing for divine worship in the celebration of Mass and the divine office.

7. Let the instructions for those preparing for communion be carefully handled especially among those who are of age so they can scrupulously fulfill the precepts.

8. Cleanliness is to be maintained in the churches and sacristy as well as on the altars and with everything that pertains to divine worship. Let the vestments be kept in chests with care and under inspection; these should be cleaned from time to time.

9. In churches where there are no baptistries, the baptismal font will be covered by some grating. The oils should be kept carefully in a cupboard under lock and key either in the sacristy or the church. There should be a shell or a silver vessel or some other suitable container for the holy water. The Baptismal registers are to be in bound books and not placed in tablets or on loose papers. The Baptismal register and the Record of Marriages are to be distinct books; each of them can serve for the whole district although it may have several pueblos as long as the pueblo involved in the Baptism or marriage is noted in the margin.

10. The Avemarias (Angelus) should be sounded morning, noon and night; also the Animas[18] should be tolled as it is done in the Province and throughout almost all New Spain. This is to be done not only in the mission cabecera but also in the pueblos of visita. The fiscales and sacristans are charged with this responsibility even though the Father may be absent.

11. The pueblos under mission administration should be visited frequently so the doctrinal instruction and good habits of the residents can be carefully reviewed. When a pueblo of visitation is large, the time spent in the visitation should be proportionate to its size. So that the Indians will be better indoctrinated everywhere, they should assist at Mass and the rest of the ministries aimed at their instruction.

12. Every year great pains should be taken to repair the houses and older churches so they will not collapse, as has happened in many places. No Father will remove anything from the house or church except with the advice and consent of the immediate superior or Visitor who will listen to the opinions of the Fathers consultor on the mission. If the proposed change involves something of importance, such as the moving of a church or house, this will not be done without prior notification to the Provincial. The change will be done according to his order and that permission will be awaited; much less will the cabecera of the district be changed without permission.

13. The inventories [*memorias*] of the furnishings of the house, church, cattle and livestock will be done clearly and distinctly. As it has been ordered, let the ledger of income and expense show what derives from Mexico as well as from other alms, if they have any, from the produce of the house or from

---

[18] The "Animas" were the indulgenced prayers recited each evening at the tolling of the church bells. These indulgences were applied to the souls of the deceased, hence the tag name of "animas."

what they have by permission from superiors. The dispersal of funds should be recorded as well as what the alms were spent for.

14. Silver spoons or vessels are not to be used, especially on our tables.

15. No Father will write or treat of any matter invclving the government of our missions with the Bishop, Governor, or Captains without first notifying his immediate superior so that he and his consultors can see what can or should be done. The immediate superior will advise the Father Visitor and await his decision. If the matter cannot wait and time does not permit prior notification, then notice will be given as soon as possible of what was resolved and what was put into practice.

16. In those districts where Indian women help in the kitchen, the kitchen door will be located on the outside of the house away from the Father's living area such that there will be no entry into that area from the kitchen. If it is necessary to carry water in, or anything else, let them be carried by the fiscales or men servants.

ZAPATA, 1678

Regulations of
Father Tomás Altamirano, 1679

[A letter of Father Provincial Tomás Altamirano[19]]

Pax Christi!

In this letter I am replying to some questions which your Reverence proposed to me in your letter of April 25, of this year, 1679, regarding the letter from Father Andrés de Zervantes.[20] I am omitting discussion of what concerns the sale of the livestock since this is no longer urgent.

Your letter was read at the Province consultation and the difficulties you proposed were reviewed; the following was decided:

1. In order to build a church in a new conversion or pueblo that is being established anew, it is not necessary to obtain the permission of the Bishop because the permission of our King and Patron who sends us on these missions is sufficient. This is proven by the fact that we see in New Spain that it is only necessary to have the permission from the King to build a church, and not from the Bishop. It is certainly true that I have written that the Bishop's permission should be sought, but this is by way of courtesy so that he will not feel offended. However, supposing that we are treating the question of jurisdiction, I say that if a new pueblo is being established, it is to be done with the permission of the Patron, who in your case is the Lord Governor of Vizcaya or his Lieutenant in that province; it would not be necessary to request permission from the Bishop.[21] I say also that it is the same in remodelling a church which has fallen in some pueblo, and if the Bishop presses some complaint against a missionary Father for doing this, the superior should call upon the Governor or the Royal Tribunal at Guadalajara. In this matter it would be well for the Bishop to proceed with gentleness and fatherly love; it was good to have pardoned him so that the work could be done with his blessing. But if he is inclined in another way, then proceed in the manner described.

---

[19] Tomás Altamirano, S.J., born 1610 in Los Lagos, Mexico, entered the Society in 1630, and was professed in 1647. He was appointed Provincial in 1676 and died in office in January, 1680.

[20] Andrés de Zervantes, S.J., born 1640 in Mexico, entered the Society in 1656, and took the final vows of a spiritual coadjutor in 1671. He worked on the missions in the Rectorate of San Ignacio on the Río Yaqui and Río Mayo. He drops from mention in the catalogs by 1708.

[21] The Bishop of Durango in 1679 was Fray Bartolomé García de Escañuela, O.F.M. The Governor of Nueva Vizcaya at this time was Don Bartolomé de Estrada y Ramírez.

Inasmuch as a different reasoning applies to chapels because, if they are in our haciendas as in the case of the one that was to be built at the hacienda of Azopece of the college of Mátape, the Rector does not need the permission of the Bishop, but of the Provincial, (and in this the Rector erred) which is according to our privileges and exemptions from the jurisdiction of Bishops. So it was when I sent permission to Father Rector Daniel Angelo so that the chapel could be built in the said hacienda because the permission he had asked from the Bishop was worthless. The Bishop was always pleased to be asked for such permissions because he was trying to insinuate his jurisdiction in opposition to our privileges and to my permission based on our exemption. The missionary Fathers do not need other chapels, and those that could be so called would be those serving the isolated rancherías; for such chapels the permission of the King who has named us Ministers of Doctrine suffices, just as he gives us bells, chalices and furnishings.

2. Regarding the second question whether the Father Visitor must countersign the registers of baptisms, marriages, and other books pertaining to the office of *doctrineros,* I say that the Bishop is correct. So, from henceforth, no Father Visitor will record his visitation in those books belonging to the church. Supposing, however, that it is ordered to have a book of income and expense for the district, our Visitor will place an account of his visitation in that book, but in no way will he sign those books which the Bishop has signed. This does not imply that the Visitor of the Society cannot or ought not know and investigate whether the district is being well administered or not, or that he should not review the baptismal registers to see if they are being done in the proper form, as the Bishop has ordered. And if the Visitor does find fault in the administration, he should advise and correct him so that on another visitation no Bishop will have anything to correct.

3. Regarding the third question whether the churches belong to Ours or to the Bishops, I say that, although the Fathers have contributed to them with their alms, silver furnishings, vestments, etc., and although the Indians have constructed them and they are for the Indians, the churches belong to the King and not to us; consequently they belong to the Bishops. And so, if we leave the missions, the church remains for the Indians, as in Tepozotlán. This should move the Fathers not to go on building up a heap of silver finery and furnishings, but rather they ought to content themselves with a suitably religious moderation in these things because his Majesty has had to declare that everything must remain for the Indians and their care even though much of it came from the Fathers' alms and the proceeds from the cattle.

4. Regarding the fourth question concerning whether the Fathers must sign thus: "I, Fulano, a curate of such and such a place," or when they are ministering in another's district, they should sign "with the permission of Father so-and-so," I declare that they shall write down "I, Fulano, a Minister of Doctrine for His Majesty," and when one serves in a foreign district (which cannot be done without the permission of its minister or the superior), they will do as the Bishop has ordered, saying "I, Fulano, with the permission of Father so-and-so the Minister of Doctrine of this district for His Majesty, baptized, etc."

5. Regarding the fifth question whether a clerical Visitor has to be admitted, in the event that the Bishop decides to send one, I say that in order to avoid contending with the said Visitor, he should be presented with the cédulas of His Majesty concerning us and also the special provisions which we have from the Royal Audiencia of Guadalajara that we are not to be visited except by the Bishop in person. But, this notwithstanding, if His Mercy wishes to proceed on his visitation of the said churches, baptismal fonts, and books, he will be received under protest that this is being done for the sake of peace. It will be understood that the concession to let him pass on his visitation will be without prejudice to the rights of the order nor in contravention to the mandates of His Majesty that we are not to be visited. In the event that he attempts anything against our rights or desires to meddle in our life and customs by inquiry, or if he should create some grievance, the Royal Proviso will be shown to the Señor Alcalde Mayor of the jurisdiction so that he can order its execution and God, Who does not abandon his poor, will work it out.

6. On the question of tithes [*diezmos*] there is little to say since the matter has been resolved in our favor, in view of the way new doors are open and new . . . [text unclear] . . . We trust that God will have the same dispatch in the review . . . and if his Excellency is contradicted and opposed, it will not be the first favor that God has done us; nor for that reason will justice, which is on our side, abandon us. Let us take care along with our religious predecessors to be the persons we ought to be, whom God cannot fail. May God preserve your Reverence for many years. Mexico. August 28, 1679.

This letter is being sent to your Reverence for its transmittal to all Fathers Superior of those missions so they can notify the missionary Fathers of two things being ordered: 1) this letter is to be transcribed into the book of Provincial regulations; 2) that none of Ours will convey to anyone what is contained in it, unless he be of the Society. Its contents are not to be discussed anywhere that it might come to the ears of an extern so that we can avoid any occasion of complaints or any conjectures on the part of anyone who might desire or who could oppose us.

Finally I say that in regard to the Californias, let the Bishop of Guadalajara declare what belongs to him and who will be declared the Bishop of the Californias, and so it has not been asserted that permission for future or possible churches there will be sought from the Bishop of Guadiana. In this matter I am unable to go further until the Viceroy declares who has competency so that we can go to him for the permissions which will be necessary, etc. I commend myself to your sacrifices. Dated as above.

Your Reverence's servant,

Tomás Altamirano

A Letter of
Father Provincial
Bernardo Pardo[22] Concerning the Manner of
Transferring Districts, 1681

Because some disorders have occurred in the missions and because some necessities have been lacking in both the missions and their houses when a missionary has been changed or has died, I have decided, with the concurrence of the Fathers Consultor, to order the following things:

1. In the event a Father is changed from one district to another or he leaves the missions for the Province, he neither can nor should dispose of the wealth that belongs to the provisions of his house or district in any way. I refer to chairs, beds, tables, chests, desks, napkins, blankets, plates, bowls, and kitchen utensils; these items may not be given away or distributed among the neighbors, as has been ordered by our Father General. With this regulation there will be no need for each missionary to set up house anew; the same thing should be observed here as in the colleges of the Province.

2. In like manner they neither can nor ought to give away cattle or pack animals [*chinchorros*] however they may have been acquired and located in the district; everything has to be left for the successor.

3. The Father who leaves his district must make an inventory of all the valuable utensils in it, of the cattle, and of all the valuables in the church; the inventory will be signed with his name and that of his successor. This will be recorded in a separate book and a copy will be sent to the superior of the mission who will share it with the Father Visitor. In the event that a successor is not present to receive and sign the inventory when he leaves, the superior of the mission will effect the transfer of all that the predecessor left in the district, which transfer will conform to the memoria of that which was inventoried and both will sign it in the prescribed manner.

5. He who supplies in any district until the proprietary arrives must understand that he is not permitted to withdraw, give away, or change any valuable item that appears on the inventory.

6. In case a missionary dies, his immediate superior will fulfill these duties, and no one else. He will examine all the valuables and anything else that remains in the houses as well as throughout the district. An inventory will be made of everything, even common and ordinary things such as clothing, white goods, etc. With the consent of the Father Visitor he can distribute

---

[22] Bernardo Pardo, S.J., born 1619 in Sevilla, entered the Society in 1636, and made his profession in 1656. He served as Provincial from 1680–83 and died in Mexico around 1685–86.

[87]

these things to deserving persons, as those who assisted the deceased in his last infirmity or as Christian and religious charity might judge best. In case there is anything of importance among the effects such as silver or other valuables, he will notify the Father Provincial so that he can dispose of it.

7. If anyone should happen to die en route to the Province, the Father Visitor who is there or someone else in his name will recover all the things that Father was carrying with him for provisions or in any other way. All these items will be inventoried and as soon as possible the Provincial will be notified and given a point-by-point report.

8. Regarding that which touches the security of conscience, according to the vow of poverty which we profess, it is good to be reminded that all the cattle and produce of our mission districts, inasmuch as they are under our authority and are our property, belong to the Province or to the college to whom the missions are applied. Only the usufruct is permitted with the kind permission of superiors, and this they will permit within the limits that religious decency allows. Wherefore, to avoid difficulties and scruples, it will be very suitable that the Father Visitor during his visitation will confer courteously and gently with each one of the Fathers about the cattle and produce which they regularly are able to sell. These conferences will concern the use of norms for the benefit of the district, its churches, and the repayment to the Province. In conformity with this and not in any other way will the current usufruct be sold.

It has seemed best to me to advise your Reverence of this so you can convey it to all the Fathers on the missions.

Your Reverence's Servant,

BERNARDO PARDO

Mexico, September 23, 1681

Regulations of
Father Visitor
Juan Almonacir, 1681-84[23]

1. I order each and every Father on the Sonora mission not to discuss Ours or our affairs with any layman. Although I know that doing this is already against the rule, still I can see that it is not being kept in many areas. Hence, since this is already a rule, I feel much more obliged to reiterate the regulation.

2. With respect to the natives, I order that no Father in any case will bind up or shear the hair of any native, man or woman, girl or boy. If by chance one of them deserves punishment by whipping, it will not exceed eight lashes. Should any native commit a more grievous crime which would call for more severe punishment, let the Fathers advise the Rector of the mission so he can determine paternally what has to be done.

3. In regard to obtaining clothing for laymen from the merchants when payment is left to the Fathers, there have arisen considerable problems. Wherefore, I order that no Father will obtain any clothing or anything else from a merchant for a layman, neither on credit nor in cash even though the laymen who desire to buy something pay in silver. The Fathers will neither extend credit to them nor permit them to enter or leave our dependencies. So that there will be no failing in this regard, I hereby revoke all permissions which the Fathers may have received from their immediate superiors in this matter. Let the Rectors know that they cannot give this permission without the order of the Father Visitor.

4. There are beggars to whom we are wont to give hospitality in our houses, whether they be priests, friars, clerics or non-clerics. They stay for weeks and even months. On the third day after their arrival they shall be notified that they are ordered to leave our houses, because if they are allowed to remain longer, notable blunders have occurred with consequent slanders against our character since after leaving they talk as it profits them and without reflection.

5. Let the Fathers make known to these beggars that I am renewing the Provincial orders and I am insisting on their observance. No alms can be given them, i.e. no silver, no mules, no animals, and nothing of use or value. They may only be supplied with bread or some other food.

6. The Fathers who might have a mill or bakery cannot sell flour nor give it away by bartering.

---

23 These did not bear any date and it is not known if they refer to Father Provincial Diego Almonacir or someone else named Juan (Diego). Juan Diego Almonacir, S.J., born 1642 in Puebla, entered the Society in 1658, and made his profession in 1678. He served on the Sinaloa mission and was Provincial from 1693–96. He died in 1706.

Regulations of
Father Provincial
Juan de Palacios, 1698

[In a letter of September 13, 1698, from Tepotzotlán Father Provincial Juan de Palacios[24] sent the following orders:]

1. Our Father General Thyrso González forwarded the permission for us to recite the office of Saint Hedwige on October 20 since this has previously been impeded by the octave of Saint Borja.

2. Our Father General has ordered that in all established missions where Sodalities of Indians are not yet formed, these will be erected and His Paternity will join them to the Primaria of the Annunciation of Rome.[25] Father Provincial says that your Reverence will notify all your missions of this order, and also that in virtue of this communique, the said Sodalities will remain affiliated, but that if it would be consoling to the Indians His Paternity will send separate letters to those who write asking his advocacy.

3. His Paternity has also advised me that he is ordering, as I am doing now, that on the missions the Fathers will be uniform in the administration of the sacraments insofar as all the ceremonies should conform to the Roman Ritual without the capricious introduction of others.

4. By order of His Paternity the admission of Indians from other districts without the permission of their proper minister is gravely forbidden.

5. Father General orders that all immediate superiors will not meddle in the temporal affairs of other districts without first notifying the Minister of them.

1703-1710

[Following these rules, but written in the same hand and noted as "other" in the margin]

Father Provincial Ambrosio Odón[26] wrote this order to Father Visitor

---

[24] Juan de Palacios Real, S.J., born 1641 in Alfaro, Spain, entered the Society in 1656, came to Mexico in 1658, and made his profession in 1678. He served as Provincial from 1696–99 and then worked as prefect of studies in the College of Saints Peter and Paul until his death in 1708.

[25] The Primaria of the Annunciation was the religious organization in Rome granted special indulgences and privileges by the Holy See. Members of the Primaria were effectively "third order" members of the Society although Jesuits struggled to keep the Society clear of such involvements. Affiliation with the Primaria was necessary to extend the privileges granted. For a discussion of its operation in Mexico, see Decorme, *Obra*, Vol. I, pp. 299-311.

[26] Ambrosio Odón, S.J., born 1641 in Saragossa, Aragon, entered the Society in 1660, and was professed in 1680. He served as Provincial from 1689–93 and again from 1702–1703. He was last reported at the College of San Ildefonso in Puebla in 1714.

Antonio Leal[27] in 1703, viz. that he was to remit to him all the outstanding debts and accounts of all the missions.

[Another in the same hand]

Father Provincial Antonio Xardón:[28]

In a letter of February 3, 1710, from Tehuacán he said this: "I am replying to your Reverence's inquiry about who is to succeed as Visitor in event of the death of the Visitor of that province. I say that this will conform to the ruling of Father Diego de Almonacir, i.e. that in the event this happens the Rector of the Sonora mission will succeed; and in the event of his death, the oldest professed Rector in the province of Sonora. If none of these are professed, then the oldest professed Father of the whole province will succeed. He will remain in office until the Provincial, having been notified, will either confirm the appointment or assign someone else. Your Reverence ought to write this ruling in the book of provincial regulations."

---

[27] Antonio Leal, S.J., born 1648 in Guadalajara, entered the Society in 1644, and made his profession in 1682. He was last reported on the Sonora missions at the Rectorate of San Francisco Xavier in 1704.

[28] Antonio Xardón, S.J., born 1656 in Mexico, entered the Society in 1671, and made his profession in 1689. He served as Provincial from 1708–1711. He is last mentioned as an *operarius* (priestly ministry) in Mexico in 1714.

Three Letters
and the Precepts of
Father Provincial A. Xardón Written to Father Visitor
F. X. Mora, 1710

[A letter of Father Provincial Antonio Xardón to Father Visitor Francisco Xavier Mora[29] from Tehuacán, February 3, 1710]

My Father Visitor Francisco Xavier Mora, Pax Christi!

On the occasion of sending Your Reverence the commission as Visitor of the Province of Sonora following the death of Father Nicolás de Villafañe,[30] I cannot omit manifesting to your Reverence the actual concern and grief that I have been caused, and the care that has been added to my ordinary duties, by the continual complaints and saddening reports that come from there about the tasteless and disgusting conduct of Ours among themselves and with the laity.

I do not know how a person can be an obedient subject unless he has at least a little love for his Holy Mother the Society and does not allow the fame she has always enjoyed to be tarnished by his own fault and carelessness. How can anyone allow her reputation to diminish which so many of our elders have gained by their great labors and vigilance? I have great confidence in Our Lord that your Reverence's watchfulness, caution, and zeal will serve to remedy the many evils which have been experienced and to prevent many others which can reasonably be feared.

From what I hear and have been told in writing, the root of the evil can easily be found and extirpated. Hence I am advising your Reverence of those points which I feel necessary that you must carefully watch:

1. First and foremost is regular religious observance inasmuch as it is compatible with life on the missions. It is certain that if the missionaries conducted themselves as they should at prayers, examen, and the rest of their spiritual exercises, as well as attending to the observance of their proper rules and regulations which have been made for the missions, there would

---

[29] Francisco Xavier Mora, S.J., born 1662 in Puebla, entered the Society in 1678, and was professed in 1696. He was the Rector of the mission in northern Sonora for several years and died in Arispe, January 7, 1720.

[30] Nicolas Villafañe, S.J., born 1638 in Celaya, entered the Society in 1654, and made his profession in 1674. He was assigned to the rectorate of San Francisco Borja, Sonora, and was last mentioned in 1708 as still at that mission.

[92]

be distinct results which would be effectively experienced. And from this it follows that:

2. I advise you secondly to shun all possible familiarities with the laity. Thus, we will avoid anyone knowing our faults or the contentions which might arise among Ours. I know that in the province there is notable laxity in this so that religious charity, that precious and esteemed jewel in the Society, is shattered so sordidly in this manner.

3. Thirdly, all possible dependence and dealings with the laity should be avoided. Those that are necessary should be kept with complete fidelity, truth, and harmony which is befitting not just religious persons but good men in general. Specifically they should not have to come here to satisfy their debts, and many missions should not be so far in debt, as I know they are, that they cause scandal and grumbling among those who know.

4. Fourth, we should maintain among Ours the love and charity which is so characteristic of the Society that we truly look on one another as brothers. In the accusations of faults we should not exceed that which our rule allows; thus we will not find ourselves plunged into confusions which customarily result from such accusations. Often reports are contradictory and so forced that they lack truth. Sometimes it has been noted that when an investigation is made maturely and prudently, which is what should be done by anyone attempting to be certain, that the original report was found to be completely false or not to be as serious as originally presented.

5. Finally what I fully desire is a care and concern for the poor Indians which is worthy of those who have left their distant homelands and the comradeship of their brothers to bring these peoples conversion, Christian education, and social and economic organization. For this it is required that they love them as children, that they teach them, and defend them even though it costs work and persecution.

I wholly desire all this in those missions where it has been languishing, and so that your Reverence may have someone to help you handle those things that may come up, I am appointing as your consultors Father Joseph Pallares[31] and Father Antonio Leal; Father Leal will also act as your Admonitor. In those instances which your Reverence judges necessary, it could be valuable to have the advice of one of the Fathers from each rectorate, according to the circumstances as they arise. I ask your Reverence to record this letter with the other provincial letters and to communicate it to all the Fathers of that province via their Rectors or in a way which might be more convenient.

God keep your Reverence.

Tehuacán, February 3, 1710.

---

[31] Joseph Pallares, S.J., born 1656 in Barcelona, Spain, entered the Society in 1674, and made his profession in 1691. He served at the mission of San Francisco Borja, Sonora, and at the College of Saints Peter and Paul in Mexico City. He is the author of *Apologia Scholastica de las Misiones de Sonora*, 1707. Pallares died at the hacienda of Calamolonga in 1718.

(This letter will be forwarded to the Father Visitor of Sinaloa after you have communicated it to the Fathers and transcribed it in the rule book.) I must be on the road so there is no time to make a copy.

Your Servant,

ANTONIO XARDÓN

[From the same Father Provincial Antonio Xardón in a letter written from Mexico, September 20, 1710]

I order the following: In case a language examination is to be offered, it will not be in a language that has been breast-fed, as they say, but one that has been learned by working with the Indians. This was ordered by the last (15th) General Congregation and formulated in an oath which is to be administered by the examiners. To wit:

I, N.N., invoking God as my witness, swear that Father N.N. is eminently qualified in the Indian language N. (which he has learned while working among the Indians) to the degree that he is fluent in familiar conversation as much as possible, and he has in this respect what the Sixth Congregation (Decree 15) and the Fifteenth Congregation (Degree 11) required for promotion to the profession of four vows.

The examiners have to be the four assigned by the Visitor. Each one has to provide four papers with his opinion duly formulated and sealed and each paper will be separately titled: "The oath of Father N.N. concerning the skill of the Indian language of Father N.N. for promotion to the profession of four vows, sent to Reverend Father General." On the fourth paper, in place of the last words, has to be written, "sent to Reverend Father Provincial." These papers will be entrusted to the Father Visitor who will remit them to Father Provincial in Mexico.

[From a letter of the same Father Provincial Antonio Xardón written from Mexico, December 12, 1710]

My Father Visitor Francisco Xavier Mora:

In order to avoid thoughtless murmuring among Ours, I am ordering that no missionary Father who finds himself injured by some layman in his vicinity, whether that injury is personal or to the lands and holdings of the district or the Indians, will stick out his nose in defense without first giving leave to the immediate superior. Through consultation he will decide what method is easiest and most effective by letter. If this does not suffice, a second consultation will be held to see if the force of justice is required. If a third instance arises and no results have been reached, the Father Visitor will be notified so he can decide if he has to bring the case to the highest places. If any Father should contravene this order, let him be summoned by his Rector who, at a junta, will impose a grave penance with the Exercises. If the case warrants, he will advise the Father Visitor so that the subject can be removed from the mission or so that he can appeal to the Father Provincial for a remedy. Your Reverence will see that this order is transcribed in the book of provincial regulations.

[From the same Father Provincial Antonio Xardón in a letter written from Puebla, December 17, 1710]

I am notifying you that a Precept has come from our Father General to the effect that none of Ours will play cards, neither with an extern nor with a subject of the house. This precept has been promulgated throughout the Province and I enjoin your Reverence to let it be known throughout your visitation. It should be recorded where similar precepts are transcribed.

Precepts of
Father Visitor General
Andrés Luque, 1714[32]

My Father Visitor Marcus Antonio Kappus,[33] P.C.

Grievous dishonor has befallen this Province of New Spain and our Mother the Society because monetary loans have been sought, particularly from the laity, sometimes with pledges of security and sometimes without them. Occasionally they have asked for money, and at other times for goods that were transferred to others. Either because of treachery or through delinquency in payment it has happened that the original creditors have raised a cry against our subject who has asked for the loan, and they claim that the order should be responsible for these debts. We have been taken to various courts on account of this and our patience and prudence are greatly tried.

Hence, to put an end to these improprieties and disorders, I hereby command in virtue of Holy Obedience that every and each Father or Brother of our Society who pertains or will pertain to this Province of New Spain, from henceforth, will not ask for a loan from externs of whatever social status or sex that would exceed the sum of 100 pesos in itself or by coalescence. This applies whether they ask the loan for themselves, whether they reloan what they would receive, or whether they ask the loan for another or others, regardless of whether they have or have not any pledges of security and regardless of any special devotion, friendship or lineage.

This first precept is understood to apply to local superiors as well as the Province Procurator and the Procurators of the rest of the colleges even when they should seek a loan for themselves or for others not as superiors or procurators, but even as ordinary citizens or private persons.

The second precept is understood to apply to the case of applying for loans for valuable furnishings for the churches, statues, or persons who will carry them at public functions, unless they have first notified the immediate superiors and satisfied them (prior to their granting permission) that the finery will be immediately returned to the owners after use, and without

---

32 Andrés Luque, S.J., born in Andalusia, was sent by Father General Miguel Angelo Tamburini as Visitor General of the Assistancy of New Spain in 1711. He discharged this office until his return to Europe in 1715, luckily surviving a shipwreck in the Bahamas on the return voyage.

33 Marcos Antonio Kappus, S.J., born 1656 in Labac, Austria, entered the Society in 1677, and made his profession in 1696. He served in the northern missions until his death at Mátape, November 30, 1717.

obligating themselves by pawning them, loaning them, or lending them to any other person.

I am placing this precept down as the Visitor of this Province. Hence it will remain perpetually in force and will be irrevocable by any other authority than our Father General who has ordered me to advise you of this precept. As a precaution that this precept will not be forgotten as well as for its usefulness, I am ordering that it be read every six months during the tridua of renovation. Moreover, I enjoin your Reverence to see that this precept is recorded in the book of regulations. I commend myself to your holy sacrifices and prayers.

Your servant,

ANDRÉS DE LUQUE

Mexico, October 13, 1714

Regulations for the Missions and Especially for Sonora, Compiled by Father Alonso de Arrivillaga, 1715[34]

1. Although Rule 21[35] orders that Ours will not communicate to laymen anything that redounds to the discredit of our missionaries, on the whole it has seemed to me best to press the execution of this rule with full vigor because of the grave failures and improprieties that have been witnessed in this particular matter, especially among the inhabitants of this province who so very easily calumniate us with lies and false testimony. Thus I add that the rule is to be observed and that under no pretext shall anyone inquire into the faults of Ours; if anyone begins to speak this way, the door is to be shut on him and the matter referred to the Superior.

2. In order to avoid every occasion of scandal and complaint in regard to profit-making and business and the rest of what is ordered in Rule 22, bargaining is strictly prohibited. As long as the Fathers have sufficient supplies for their consumption they cannot bargain for their maintenance under any pretext or title by selling what they have gotten from the harvest. I enjoin the superiors to guard over this matter; they are not to fail to punish severely whoever fails in this because such a practice is so detrimental to us by occasioning scandals; nor does it conform to Holy Poverty.

3. While leaving Rule 23 in force as it pertains to mayordomos, I add that they will not live inside the mission compound with their wives or with any other women, nor will they live alongside the Father's house. And the Reverend Fathers will not visit the women even out of courtesy except in the case that Holy Charity dictates otherwise.

4. Concerning Rule 48 that Ours will not carry weapons, let the following words appear at the end: "Upon notice that a remedy cannot be applied, the superiors are obliged to command compliance by precept as it is evident to me that there is failure in this. I am leaving this regulation in force and I will consult in Mexico if it is necessary to command this under precept."

5. Because that same Rule 48 orders the observance of religious decency, interior as well as exterior, I charge your reverences with its exact observance, e.g. perhaps some buttons have been replaced and although they may be false

---

[34] Alonso de Arrivillaga, S.J., born 1650 in Guatemala, entered the Society in 1665, and made his profession in 1681. He served as Provincial from 1711–15 during the visitation of Andrés Luque. He is last mentioned as directing the building of the Casa Profesa in Mexico in 1720.

[35] Rule 21 of Hernando Cabrero, 1662. See page 70.

gold, they can still cause disedification. I say the same thing about handkerchiefs, snuff boxes, colored scarfs, buttons or buckles on shoes, silver clasps on capes, lace on birretas, or in sum, anything that does not conform to our state or custom in the Province.

6. The Fathers are not to involve themselves in any way in capturing Indians who have fled their masters so they can be returned to their mines or haciendas. Because of the excessive punishment that some are wont at times to give these poor people, which can bring about their death or serious injury, we ought to involve ourselves beforehand in procuring their complete exoneration.

7. There is to be no omission in regards to the juntas as has been ordered in Rule 28. At the juntas the superiors will correct the failures they have noticed in the manner of dress and anything else that could be detrimental.

8. It seems fitting to me that the subject who would be at the mission of Mátape with the title of Rector ought to recognize as his superior the Rector at the mission of San Borja and he ought to assist at the juntas like the rest; this is the way it has been done in the Tarahumaras where the Rector of Guejotitlán, although he is a rector, is subject to the superior of the mission of the Nativity of Our Lady.

9. Inasmuch as I have noticed that some have a facility in failing to tell the truth, which is a despicable fault even in laymen, and that others have a facility to talk about Ours to their serious detriment and loss of reputation, I intend to say no more here than to remind them of the serious obligation they have to observe in this matter, i.e., the law of God. I will say no more because I am addressing myself to rational people.

10. Father Visitor General Andrés de Luque in a letter of September 1, 1714, having learned of the inordinate allotments which were being made by Ours to their parents and relatives, ordered that no missionary would allot anything to his parents, brothers, and especially his sisters, despite their poverty, up to the value of 25 pesos annually. This ruling also applies to Ours because the practice is so contrary to Holy Poverty. I am advising and commanding everyone to take account of what they are doing so they will not fall into this temptation. The money would be better employed in improving the churches, their furnishings, or those items which pertain to divine worship. If all this is in good condition, then they ought to allot this money toward the welfare of the province as their common mother who has indebted herself in great measure for their benefit. And I would add also that they ought to look out for the welfare of the poor Indians. The first alms should be to those whom we owe in justice because all that we have has been acquired by their work and sweat; to observe this ruling let us not undertake inordinate labors and copious plantings.

11. Some have been so interested in temporal gains that they have obliged the Indians to continual labor to the extent that the Indians have been unable to attend to their own crops; thus the laymen have had reason to calumniate us regarding the Indian's situation and even to claim that we have enslaved the natives along with other serious charges. Therefore, I strictly forbid that the Indians will be obliged to work except for the first three days of the week

or during harvest time when, if the work should be interrupted, the whole crop might be endangered; the work to which they are obliged is to be precise, such as the repair of the churches, which ought to be repaired now throughout Sonora or ruin will otherwise befall them. In all earnestness I charge the superiors to see to the exact observance of this regulation so the laymen and the Indians can see that we seek only their souls. Since the Fathers should be aware of this, the superiors will see that this is read at all the juntas together with the rest of the regulations which have been repeatedly ordered.

12. Inasmuch as the expenditures for chocolate have been noticed as the largest outlay on the missions, I enjoin that there will be moderation and careful selection among the persons to whom it is given.

13. In regard to Rule 3, since it is evident that twelve pack mules are not enough for the missionary who returns to the Province from Sonora, I am permitting the missionaries to take up to twenty-four, but that number is not to be exceeded. The rest of that regulation remains in force. On the trip the Fathers may take only what is necessary for their own sustenance and for payment of their servants, but this is not to exceed five hundred pesos in silver since there have been grave excesses in this matter.

14. Because there has been an abuse in these provinces of the missionaries interfering in the removal of the infant from the baptismal font, I strictly command that this is not to be done, as the Ritual states, because of the many improprieties that can occur. If it becomes necessary, a precept will be laid down. Let those who have recently arrived in their districts be advised that they cannot permit two godmothers and godfathers at baptisms, as is quite clear in the Ritual; I am advising this so that the Bishop will not find the fault in the registers, as I have found. Likewise, it is not necessary to wait eight days before baptizing people. When children are brought for baptism, the missionary will perform the baptism without delay. The missionary should not baptize with water that is not consecrated, except in case of necessity, because this is contrary to the ruling by the Council of Trent; there has been laxity in this regard.

15. Furthermore, I command and enjoin that Ours will not participate in fandangos at weddings, anniversaries, and much less at comedies.

16. It is very important to observe what is commanded by precept from Rome, especially that no one, particularly missionaries, dare write letters or reports to the Viceroys, Audiencias, Governors, etc. The superiors will be responsible to see that no one who acts to the contrary will escape punishment.

17. In the matter of writing and keeping letters many serious improprieties have been observed. Since, as we are mortals, the written word remains, letters can serve as the father of rumors and the seedbed of discord. Wherefore, I beseech you in the bosom of Jesus Christ, that whoever has any such letters will hereupon burn them (as some have already done). In the future the Fathers should take a careful look at what they are writing because *littera scripta manet* and they can break charity apart in various ways which is something we should take very much to heart in our Society which is after all a Society of love.

18. I am making it the superiors' responsibility to know if each district

has a set of the regulations; if not, they shall order one to be made and the Fathers are ordered to read them every three months. Permissions are to be renewed every four months as long as no insuperable impediments occur such as high water, etc., which is similar to the practice of renewing permissions monthly in the colleges. Thus, not only will Holy Poverty be looked after but also obedience since they will have the proper recourse to their superiors.

19. Let each district have a copy of the prayers written down in its own language. In this way the *temastianes* will not change them and the words will not be corrupted through the passage of time, nor will the newer Fathers who come find themselves beset by doubts and scruples. Then, too, this will help them learn.

20. Only those who deserve our hospitality by blood or authority will be invited to our feasts. They will be served with what the Indian cooks have prepared without permitting the Spaniards to meddle in the feast, which only serves as an excuse for expense and gossip.

21. Finally, in order to maintain charity and devotion toward our deceased brothers, because I have noticed some carelessness in this regard, I order the superiors to notify the Fathers of their visitation and rectorate immediately about the death of one of Ours so that there will be no delay in suffrages. The same care will be taken to notify the Province as well as the Visitors of the other missions. They will compile a letter of edification as is the custom of our Society. When the juntas are convened, let them take care that the assembled Fathers will have brought their annual reports [*puntas de annua*] so each suitable topic can be coordinated and translated into Latin.

I hereby confirm and approve all these regulations, as they stand, with the approbation of the consultors. I am adding to these regulations only that I prohibit the playing of lottery, or little cards, which Ours are in no way to play.

ALONSO DE ARRIVILLAGA

Mexico, September 5, 1715.

[Attached in another hand]

The missions which the King has endowed in this Province and Visitation of Sonora are thirty; it is fitting to know:

Onapa, Arivechi, Saguaripa, Movas, Onavas, Cumuripa, Tecoripa, Mátape; these constitute the rectorate of San Borja.

Ures, Opodepe, Cucurpe, Acontzi, Banamichi, Arispe, and Cuquiarachi; these constitute the rectorate of San Xavier.

Baseraca, Bavispe, Bacadeguachi, Guazavas, Oposura, and Batuco; these constitute the rectorate of the Holy Martyrs.

San Ignacio, Caborca (vacant), Tubutama, San Xavier del Bac, Guevavi, Santa María Suamca, Sariqui, Sonoita, and Cocospera, which is the same as the mission of the Sobaipuris; these constitute the rectorate of Dolores.

Over and above these thirty missions there are three endowed in the Pimería Alta; these are: Atí, Tucson, and another among the Sobaipuris. All thirty-three are in charge of the Father Procurator of the missions who provides for them with their alms.

Father Provincial has ordered that the Fathers Visitor of this Province will annually collect the certificates that the Fathers have made the Exercises and read the decrees. They will merely notify the Provincial by letter that the juntas have been held and that the Fathers have made their Exercises and read the decrees.

A Letter of Father Provincial
Gaspar Rodero, 1716[36]

My Father Visitor Marcos Antonio Kappus, P.C.

My predecessor justly ordered that in no mission or college of this Province will an educated [*de razon*] woman live or be a servant under any pretext. As this is extremely important, your Reverence should insist on it; notify me whether this is being done in all the missions, and if need be, place down a precept.

Some have given grave scandal by selling to laymen those things which they have received through the *memorias* of their alms or things which they have sought elsewhere by other means (the merchants are grumbling about it). Therefore, I order in virtue of Holy Obedience and under pain of mortal sin that none of the Fathers missionary will sell anything or ask or permit a layman to do the same for them. In case there is some surplus or a danger of loss if the goods are stored, the Fathers will notify the Father Visitor so he can decide what is most just and suitable in this regard.

Many missions have asked the provincial office for the whole of their alms although the alms have not been paid by the Royal Treasury for the past two years. Their need is poorly verified because of the excesses they have gone to in providing for the beggars who go about these provinces. One of them, who begged only a few days, bragged that he had received 5000 pesos from those missions alone. Such liberality is exorbitant and creates a grave prejudice against all the missionary Fathers because it justifies the judgment which we fear His Majesty has nearly reached to cease to give alms to many missions because they have not only enough for themselves but also for others. If an effective and just defense against these claims is to be made, from now on we should not give away anymore; it has seemed best to me that I set down a precept under Holy Obedience, and I am now so doing, that no missionary will exceed twelve pesos, in goods or silver, in giving an alms to any one of those who traffic in this ministry. The missionaries will also order them at the same time that they will not remain in our houses for more than three days unless there is a very serious reason to grant a dispensation from this ruling.

---

[36] Gaspar Rodero, S.J., born 1669 in Madrid, entered the Society in 1684, and made his profession in 1702. He served as Provincial from 1715–19 and from 1725–26 until he was called to Spain in June, 1726, to become the Procurator of the Indies.

Your Reverence will inform all your subjects about these precepts and notify me that you have done so. I pray that your Reverence will be zealous beyond your deserts in a matter that is so important to the good reputation of our apostolic ministries. May Our Lord keep you many years which I desire and for which I pray.

Your Reverence's servant,

GASPAR RODERO

Tepotzotlán, August 19, 1716.

A Compendium of Instructions
From Father Provincial
Joseph de Arjó[37] to
Father Juan de Guendulain[38] and Afterward to
Father Joseph de Echeverria[39]
for the General Visitation
of the Missions

Chapter One: The jurisdiction of Father Visitor General

1. I hereby concede to Father Juan de Guendulain and to his successors all my powers in either forum, except that of admission into or dismissal from the Society, and I restrict the making of contracts which could result in hardships on the missions or colleges of his jurisdiction. In everything else I communicate to him all my powers so they may be used as those of the Ordinary over superiors and subjects in the provinces and colleges of Sinaloa, California, Sonora, Tarahumara, Tepehuán, the Sierra, Nayarit, Parral, and Chihuahua. The said superiors and subjects will have recourse to the Fathers Visitor General and not to the Provincials except in extraordinary cases but never before the execution of what the Fathers Visitor General have ordered.

2. The Visitor General will take care to leave the work to the Visitors and Rectors, and when they are fit instruments, the Visitor General of these said superiors will be empowered for the execution of their own determinations.

3. When a Visitor or Rector of a college, present or future, dies, his Reverence will name the most fitting subject to that post whether he be from the same province as the deceased or another one. For the triennial government of the colleges and visitation districts, his Reverence will submit during the last year of their terms the names of three subjects for each province and college, and each Rector and Visitor will do the same for his province, for which his Reverence will instruct them in what has been ordered in Chapter 17 of the General Rules.[40]

---

[37] Joseph de Arjó, S.J., born 1663 in Aragon, entered the Society in 1678, and was professed in 1696. He served as Provincial from 1722–25; he died at the College of San Andrés, Mexico, in 1736.

[38] Juan Guendulain, S.J., born 1680 in Oaxaca, entered the Society in 1696, and made his profession in 1715. He was named the first permanent Visitor of the northern missions. He died in Puebla, July 31, 1748.

[39] Joseph Echeverria, S.J., born 1689 in San Sebastian, Cantabria, entered the Society in 1704, and made his profession in 1721. The last mentioned of him in the catalog occurs in 1751.

[40] The General Rules refer to a set of administrative regulations pertaining to the Assistancy of New Spain which have not been located in the extant documents.

4. It would seem more fitting that the Visitor General, having made his solicitations before he informs and appoints the subjects in the province, will make the appointments, not as formerly, but at the time when the Rectors are completing their triennial terms.

5. The informants have to be four in number and for the *informationes*[41] that come here they will be: 1) your Reverence, 2) the Visitor of each province, 3 and 4) the eldest rectors, and in their absence whomever the Visitor appoints. For the *informationes* for the mission Rectors the Visitor of the province and the three Rectors will make the reports; if the Rectors are lacking, then one or two of the eldest persons will report.

6. When there are reasons to suspend a mission Rector, the Visitor General will do so with the advice and opinion of the consultors of the Province to which the subject pertains. Visitors and Rectors of college will not be deposed from their office without the approval of the said Father Provincial.

7. Any custom to the contrary notwithstanding, I am taking away from the particular Visitors the faculty to designate a mission for new arrivals and also to change men on the mission from one region to another. These faculties, since they are properly the Provincial's, I communicate solely to the Visitor General who is not to permit any contrary practice except in the event of grave urgency and difficult recourse.

8. The Visitor General, by his right of Ordinary, can change any subject anywhere in his jurisdiction. If necessary, he can send subjects back to Guadiana and Guadalajara as on deposit. He will send the required report to the respective college Rector and a letter to Father Provincial outlining the causes which obliged him to do so.

9. The office and jurisdiction of the Visitor General begin immediately with his entry into any mission province whatsoever; they will remain in force until a successor is actually in possession in one of the said provinces. Not only will the missionaries be subject to the Visitor General but also anyone entering or leaving the missions as long as they are within any mission province whatsoever.

10. The Visitor of the province in which the Visitor General actually is will always be designated as the Admonitor to the Visitor General. The consultors will be: 1) the Admonitor; 2, 3, and 4) the three oldest rectors in the province or, in their absence, one or two of the subjects who have been the longest in the province. This is understood to apply to that which pertains to the particular government of each province.

11. Moreover, business which is common to all the missions or which is of a very serious nature will be taken under consultation, even though only by writing, with the four Visitors closest to the place where the Visitor General actually is. The opinion of others nearby who can speak with certitude will be listened to.

---

[41] *Informationes* are secret reports requested from members of the Society on the general character, ability, and health of men being considered for any particular work or promotion in the Society.

Chapter Two: Concerning Contributions for the Maintenance of the Father
Visitor General

12. I order the Visitor General to have a book or tablet in which he will record from now on how much he is given for travelling expenses and how much he receives from Ours for his maintenance and other expenses. When his office is finished, he will give an account to the Provincial from this book, or to whomever the Provincial will appoint to review the expenditures of his term of office.

13. Since the presence of the Visitor General in the missions and colleges of his jurisdiction has to be almost continual, let the missions and colleges assist him with everything he needs by way of food and supplies which will be required for his journey when he leaves for another place. With that, it would seem that the Visitor General will only need the means to pay for his clothing, transportation, salaries for his servants, paper, chocolate and some other extraordinary item that he might want to offer.

14. I have determined that if he needs mules or horses, he will ask for them from the missions who have an abundance of this kind. He will apply them to his office and record them in the account book. He can have one or two foot-servants on continual salary and he will take from one mission or another the rest of the servants he needs. For these and other expenses the Father Visitor can ask the missions what they can give as a contribution for what his Reverence judges necessary without his having to wait until the time of the visitation, although it would be better if he sought the contribution at the time he visits each mission.

15. Beyond what has been said (viz. that the Visitor General have an account book which he will produce on request) I order each one of the Visitors General of the missions in virtue of Holy Obedience and under pain of mortal sin that none of Ours who pertain to the jurisdiction of the said Visitors General will receive silver, money, valuables, merchandise, animals, or any other products, or generally speaking anything which the aforementioned subjects might give the Visitors General (and this also applies to the Visitor's companion) as a friendly present, gift, birthday remembrance, or under any other title which would not fall under a contribution as mentioned above or under the obligation of the Visitor's account.

16. In order to prevent this even more effectively, I order in virtue of Holy Obedience that the said Visitors General will not accept such things even though Ours might give them by means of a third party. If the Visitors were ignorant of what they received, they will make restitution. Granted these restrictions, I want both the Visitors as well as their subjects to know that I do not prohibit those religious presents which before God and man are not tainted with the appearance of profiteering or gain, e.g. to receive some bezoar stones, trinkets, *contrayerbas*, napkins, blankets, bits of chocolate and similar things; I do not prohibit this as long as they are not in a vast quantity, but as one would normally receive. They are not to be sold except for the uses of the said Fathers Visitor or for religious gifts to whoever might desire or want them. On the other hand, the said Visitors should understand that the items herein excepted are included in the precept and come

under the same serious obligation of not being received or retained after they are received.

17. Moreover, I order the Visitors General that they will not empower any alms to be collected or remitted for any of our houses or colleges, nor for any pious work or needy persons without the opinion of Father Provincial; otherwise such occurrences could weaken the executive effectiveness in the major superior.

Chapter Three: Concerning Spiritual Administration

18. It has come to my attention that some Fathers, although they know the language of their flocks, scarcely preach to them even once. Hence, it is fitting that the Visitor General as well as the rest of the superiors not tolerate such omission without punishing those at fault. They will oblige their subjects to preach a moral exhortation or give a doctrinal talk to the Indians in the church every Sunday for at least a half hour; this may be after the Gospel or after the Mass. Except in the case of illness, they will not accept excuses so that anyone who is frequently careless will not be exonerated.

19. Many Indian tribes, although they have been reduced to the Faith for many years, still have the fault of not being prepared to receive their annual communion or even viaticum. Their ministers, and not less the superiors, have the serious obligation in conscience to see that each one does his part in making certain that the Indians will be taught what is necessary for the reception of the divine sacrament. Although religious ministers are convinced that there are tribes incapable of the necessary disposition, I consider this the devil's trickery prejudicing their salvation. Wherefore, the missionaries will frequently bring up in their sermons and conferences the proposed topic in order to instruct the understanding and dispose the will of their flocks. They will continue to give annual communion and viaticum to those who are well instructed; in this way they will profit from the sacraments and their example will dispose others to do the same.

20. In some places the bad practice of carrying the sick to the church for the reception of the holy oils and for confession has been introduced. The excuse has been that there is no danger because these peoples do not know how to undergo their worst sicknesses without taking the sick from their houses and placing them in the sun and air. Despite that, I consider this practice an intolerable abuse which has been introduced out of laziness. Hence, I am enjoining the superiors to see that it is rooted out.

21. Not a little damage has been done to the spiritual welfare of the Indians when their ministers display impatience with them in the confessional or when they treat them harshly in ordinary matters; the Fathers should keep their feelings very much under control in common affairs. Wherefore, the superiors shall keep an eye on this and they will admonish and correct those who treat the Indians with a charity that is less than their tenderness demands. The lack of consideration by some missionaries is to be diminished as when they oblige the Indians to work or to suffer annoying delays as though they were aspiring to establish entailed estates.

22. Some missions, even after many years, still have no church. I am hereby ordering that where there are none the superiors are to urge their

subjects to build them so that at least in the main pueblo of the mission there will be an ample church which befits the number of the faithful. In each visita there should be a decent church or chapel for the neighboring people.

23. Some missionaries assert the lack of churches or some other frivolous pretext as the reason why they do not visit the pueblos unless they are called to hear confessions. From this neglect has arisen the problem that a great portion of the faithful throughout the year do not have Mass, instructions, nor confidence in the Fathers for want of communication. Therefore I am ordering that all the missionary Fathers who have pueblos of visitation will celebrate a Sunday Mass in each visita every month; they will notify those who have to hear the Mass so that they will know where they should go to assist. The Father will remain in the pueblo where they have chosen to say Mass two or three days (unless necessity calls them elsewhere) in order to better acquaint themselves with their flocks. They should also attend to their spiritual and temporal needs and inform themselves about what pertains to the children's instruction and the vigilance of the governors in punishing delinquents to avoid scandals.

24. Another point of bad administration is the tepidity of some who have become accustomed to not saying Mass except only on feast days or at best on Saturdays when a crowd has gathered for a Mass in honor of the Virgin. I know in some places the inclemency of the weather, hot or cold, has served as an excuse for so much laziness; but without being rash I suspect the root of this will be a tepidity even worse than laziness itself. Therefore I charge the superiors to inspire their subjects, who are afflicted this way, with gentleness; and if this is not enough, with firmness so they will be shaken from the laziness that touches on scandal and dispose themselves to celebrate Mass more frequently, thus giving good example to their neighbors and parishioners.

Chapter Four: The Study of the Language

25. The ministry of our missionaries is inseparable from the obligation of instructing their flock spiritually. This cannot be done if they lack even moderate skill in using the language. It has come to my attention that, as it has been up to now, there are missionaries who even after being in the missions for years have not learned the language. They have contented themselves in writing down questions for confession; still others have preached to their parishioners in Spanish on the excuse that most or all of them understand it.

26. I order your Reverence to watch over the individual Visitors and Rectors in each province so that they put into practice what I have ordered in this regard. Let it be known that new missionaries, after a reasonable time (corresponding to each one's capacity) are obliged to preach to the Indians in the church in the presence of the said Visitors and Rectors. They will repeat this exercise until the superiors are satisfied that they can use the language of the administration with such skill that everyone's conscience will rest at ease.

27. If at the first of these examinations the subject is found to be lacking skill, taking into account the time and his ability, I order the Visitors and

Rectors not to let the subject pass without giving him some grave penance; they are to notify your Reverence of the failure and the punishment. If the subject fails at the second examination, a more severe punishment will be imposed under the same above conditions. If the subject is examined a third time in the prescribed form and he culpably fails, I order your Reverence and the Visitors of each province to remove the subject immediately from the mission even though there be a great lack of workers. The subject will be placed in another mission where he will be accompanied by someone who knows the language well so he can learn it from him. In no case is any mission to be placed in the subject's care until he knows the language of its Indians.

28. Moreover, I warn your Reverence, and your Reverence will warn all the Visitors, that any subject who is now in the missions and any who may come in the future will not be admitted to the grade of the Professed or Formed Coadjutor unless he is found to be skilled in the grade expressed above for administering to the Indians; such profession or formation is not according to my will, nor will it be according to that of my successors. Neither your Reverence nor any other of the individual superiors in these provinces will accept such grades until the superiors of those to be advanced in grade are certain of their skill in the language.

29. Regarding the subjects who are already long established in the missions, if any of them do not possess a suitable skill in the language, I charge your Reverence personally and by means of the Visitors to employ all means, both gentle and firm, to assure that they acquire this skill; you may also use the remedy, if it becomes necessary, of removing them from their missions and replacing them with others while they are qualifying. This will remove the satisfaction of being where they are so that the public examinations can be made by persons whom your Reverence completely trusts.

30. In some missions the parishioners speak different languages. Although it would be commendable for the minister to know them all, the superiors should be satisfied that the minister has learned the most common and generally understood one.

31. It is sometimes noted that changing a subject from mission to mission also involves a change of language. Since it is so difficult for a subject to learn a new language in a short time, it happens that the door is almost closed to such changes which could be compensated for if they became necessary by transfer to another distant mission which speaks the same language. In spite of this the Visitor General can order the contrary in a case of very grave necessity.

32. It is most lamentable, as often happens, that when a Father is recently come to a mission, he finds his predecessors lacked the foresight to leave him anything about the Indian language, even some notes on what they had learned about it; the result is that there is no little difficulty for the Fathers to make prompt use of the language. Therefore the Fathers Visitor at the time of their visitation will ask each mission what has been done in this regard. They will take care to see that the Fathers leave one another better information about the languages, compiling grammars, vocabularies, confessionaries, catechisms, sermons and general observations.

Chapter Five: Concerning Some Faults Which Occur in
Some Missionaries

33. Failures in charity are at times very noticeable. This requires great vigilance among the superiors; they will be firm in punishing failures, executing to the letter what I have ordered in the circular letter cited: Let everyone know that whoever is seriously delinquent in this matter has to go to one of the colleges and make the Exercises for eight days together with the other penances which the Visitor deems suitable.

34. Usually these failures in charity stem from too great a familiarity with the laymen. These men employ much liberty in speech and gossip thus estranging the spirits of some missionaries from the others. Then they compel them to disclose their weaknesses and the faults of their brothers so that once the laymen have heard about them, they are publicized everywhere. It is fitting that everyone reflect on the serious harm that inconsiderate speech causes; this pertains just as much to private persons as to missionaries in general.

35. On the contrary, there are some missionaries who write and speak arrogantly about laymen's scandals, whether among themselves or between laymen, on the excuse that these are public affairs or on the pretext of being a "defense." They seldom take note that they speak with little foundation and are giving an occasion of scandal without hope of benefit and with distinct harm. Such liberty demands no less an effective remedy than the preceding fault.

36. Some missionaries, and very zealous ones at that, have complained that their letters which were destined for superiors have been maliciously detained. I am not persuaded that this is the case, but, nevertheless, it is fitting to remind all that this is a serious and privileged matter in the Society. Moreover, let the superiors dispatch such letters promptly and securely.

37. The Fathers Visitor will see that the missionaries keep the baptismal registers, and books of marriage and burial in the proper form. During the time of visitation they will review the books; this pertains to the Visitor General as well as the individual Visitors.

Chapter Six: The Temporal Administration of the Missions

38. Let an inspection be made of how the temporal administration is progressing.

39. I order your Reverence to make certain that each mission has a ledger which clearly shows the income and expense. Your Reverence and the individual Visitors will review it during the visitations so that all which was earned or spent is accounted for.

40. When anyone leaves a mission for another, let him account for all he leaves in the church, house, chapel, etc. He will sign the entry which he makes along with whoever receives it, which should be the Rector or someone in his place.

41. The ministers are not permitted to provide a different mission with anything that properly belongs to their own without the permission of the Visitor General.

42. It is my will that neither your Reverence nor any other Visitor give

permission to remove anything from a vacant mission; taking into consideration the state of the petitioner's mission and the need he expresses, it could be ordered that he be given an alms if that be available.

43. Transferring personnel from one mission to another ordinarily does not happen without affecting the temporalities of a mission; hence, while we prescind from the themes of Chapter Four, the changing of subjects from one mission to another should be avoided as much as possible.

44. I order that your Reverence is not to permit a mission to indebt itself beyond what is necessary even though it might be for the furnishing of the church; far less for other things.

45. Missionaries are wont to go into debt to protect Spanish families, their mayordomos, and other distant people who ask their help. The superiors are to take a strong stand to eradicate this unsuitable practice. The missions are not prohibited from retaining mayordomos at a just wage as long as they do not suck blood out of the Indians.

Chapter Seven: Concerning the Manner of Correction
                and Denunciation

46. Recent news obliges me to set down some penances for specific faults and to order your Reverence to adhere to them:

47. First, what has been commanded in Regulation 26 and following in regard to the culpable delay in learning the Indian language is to be observed. Second, when a subject has been given well-founded notice about his personal conduct, he will be punished severely; if he still fails to correct himself, let him be sent back to some college where he will stay for six months without going out for anything, even to hear confessions.

48. Superiors should be zealous that Ours will not permit women to come into their houses; nor will Ours frequent the houses of women. Superiors will punish anyone delinquent in this regard according to what I have written in the circular letter at the order of Father General.

49. It would be good for the superiors to realize that they can scarcely believe denunciations from the laymen. Among the educated people it has been found that they irreparably damage the reputation of the priests; and among the Indians, it has been found that they act out of hate and vengeance because they were beaten at the order of the Fathers.

Chapter Eight: Miscellaneous Other Things

50. It has often happened that when the Visitors request subjects to restaff vacant missions, the subjects have failed to be sent because of the lack of means. I am ordering that when a mission is vacated, the Visitor of that province will take out three hundred pesos in silver or money which will be sent to Father Provincial so a subject can promptly be sent.

51. The missions which are less prosperous are to be assigned to those subjects recently arrived from the province. If less demanding missions are vacant, they should be given to the older missionaries as long as they know the language and there is no objection.

52. Taking care of the poorer missions, such as Nayarit and Topia, is entrusted to the Visitor General. They will be helped as much as possible, but he will not ask for alms without taking care of the poor missions and paying for the receipt of the subjects sent there.

53. Your Reverence will order, during his visitations of the missions, that each one of Ours will remove from the formulas of the *informatio ad gradum* as much as has been commanded by the Sixth Decree of the ninth Congregation.[42] In the colleges the Rectors will delete this; they can write down the ruling in the book of regulations.

54. In the circular letter cited, I have advised the missionaries of Reverend Father General's complaint regarding the poor method used in the annual reports. Let your Reverence see that the Visitors and Rectors receive detailed instructions in each province so that each province distinctly lists its rectorates, missions; the number of pueblos, marriages, bachelors, children, baptisms, deaths, pagans converted; the number of churches; progress in the Faith; devotional exercises; rare happenings, etc.; and also a brief resume of the temporalities.

55. The Visitor General will promote the colleges of Sinaloa and Chihuahua. He will provide for a boarding school to be erected in Sonora where there will be provision for Spaniards to reside. The Fathers in Sonora will be consulted about this plan and when your Reverence has reviewed the matter, steps will be taken to initiate the work for which the missions may be asked to contribute.

56. Provision should be made for the missionary colleges to maintain their rents and to be improved so that the colleges can maintain at least six missions whereby a great deal of benefit will accrue to the missions. Your Reverence and the individual Visitors will keep watch over the Rectors so they administer everything in their charge with more moderation, especially in regard to the missionaries who permit more liberality in spending for their children.

57. Your Reverence will convey to all the Fathers personally and later at a consultation of the consultors of each province that the colleges of Parral and Chihuahua, and in time the college of Sonora, will become the rectorates of the missions and their Rectors, the mission superiors, as the case is in Sinaloa. Each college will take over four or six of the closest missions, thus providing for a new design of rectorates for the remaining missions.[43]

---

[42] *Informationes ad gradum* are reports made prior to the admission of any member of the Society to a "higher grade." The most serious of these reports is made before admission to final vows when a man is given either the profession of four vows or admission as a spiritual coadjutor.

The Ninth General Congregation met in Rome from December 13, 1649, through February 23, 1650. Decree 6 cautioned informants on the seriousness of the report especially as it concerned the need for virtues beyond mediocrity.

[43] This is a curiosity appearing here as a Rule because the Colleges on the frontier never took over the mission rectorates. This revision of the system as stated here must be understood only as a plan that never materialized.

58. If the establishment of these rectorates poses no difficulty, your Reverence will go ahead; if there are serious things that oppose it, your Reverence will advise me of everything and forward your opinion.

59. Many things contained in this instruction have been previously foreseen by the regulations from Father General and other superiors. Nevertheless, the actual knowledge which I possess moves me to propose them to your Reverence for the good government of your office. I charge your Reverence to collect throughout all the missions whatever precepts and regulations have been sent, and while your Reverence remains there, with a copy, someone should come to Mexico so that it can be seen if a briefer extract would be suitable.

60. Your Reverence will promulgate to each missionary whatever is contained in these instructions so that no one can plead ignorance. Neither Visitors, Rectors, nor subjects are excused from what your Reverence directs in virtue of this said instruction, etc.

JOSEPH DE ARJÓ

Addenda: The formulas for the *informatio ad gradum* or *ad gubernandum* are followed by the order that the *informationes* will be sent to Father Provincial; only the *informationes* for mission Rectors will be sent to the Visitor General.

The precept of not receiving the position of Visitor General is understood of his companion who holds the office of secretary in the same form.

JUAN DE GUENDULAIN

Precepts Which Were
Found in the Missions

1. A Precept of Father Luis del Canto:[44] In virtue of Holy Obedience I order that no one will send silver to anyone for the support of their missions; it can only be sent to the Province Procurator. And I further declare that no superior can give permission to the contrary because of the serious consequences which can result and which have weighed against the missions. Any such action is in violation of the vows of poverty and obedience. (1683–86).

2. From the same: Spaniards will not be charged for funeral services, but they may freely donate if they so desire.

3. From the same: I order that there will be a ledger of income and expense wherein they will record the silver earned from the crops; separately they will record what was made on cattle, sheep, horses, mules, etc. They will also record the quantities spent. (Father Provincial Juan de Almonacir declared that this precept applied to those who had much livestock, but not to those whose herds were less than 1000.)

4. From the same: Each Father will write the Provincial at the end of the year about the money he has earned from these activities and also about what he has spent.

5. A Precept of Father General Thyrso González and confirmed by Father General Miguel Angelo:[45] Expensive buildings and costly furnishings will not be undertaken as long as the missions are in debt. If these furnishings have been commissioned to be made from benefactors' donations while there are debts, the missionaries will not take on the responsibility of collecting or utilizing such donations except in very small sums.

6. No one shall be punished by more than eight lashes.

7. A Precept of Father Provincial Bonifaz and confirmed by Father Provincial Antonio Díaz: No one will undertake new expeditions into pagan territory without the Father Visitor's prior notification to Father Provincial and the arrival of the documented answer.

8. No one will play cards either with Ours or with externs.

9. No one can work at mining.

---

[44] Luis del Canto, S.J., born 1634 in Antequera, Spain, entered the Society in 1649. He worked in the northern mission for sixteen years prior to his term as Provincial from 1683–86. He died in Mexico, December 26, 1687.

[45] Miguel Angelo Tamburini, S.J., Praepositus General of the Society, 1706–1730.

10. A precept of Father Provincial Andrés Nieto: If anyone knows that the prohibition against card-playing has been violated, he will notify the Provincial.

11. From the same: The same Father Provincial Nieto extended the precept against writing the Viceroy, Governors, Bishops without the permission of the Father Visitor and first sending him the letter to include also any Oidores whomsoever.

12, 13, 14. No one can indebt himself for more than 500 pesos. No one shall have a woman cook, whether Indian, Spaniard or mulatto. No one shall have a mayordomo.

15. A Precept of Father Provincial Luis del Canto: The Fathers will not have any brother or other relative in their district; nor will they receive any relative into their houses except that he be treated like any other layman. The Fathers will not give them anything either directly or indirectly, nor will they entrust anything to them. The Fathers will not send either directly or indirectly any Indian to work in a mine or as a servant. The Fathers will not favor their relatives by extending credit to merchants or any other persons involved in buying and selling clothing or anything else. They will not remit or dispose of anything either directly or indirectly that touches on the support of their persons, houses or haciendas.

16. A Precept of Reverend Father General: Neither refined women or Indians will serve the missionaries inside the house.

17. A Precept of Father Provincial Gaspar Rodero: No one will sell anything that has been acquired by alms, nor will anyone permit a layman to sell them except that they might otherwise be lost. The Fathers must ask the Visitor what disposition he felt was most just and fitting in this matter.

18. A Precept of Father Provincial Francisco de Arteaga: No one will possess knowledge about mining either directly or indirectly; even if his intention is to have a general knowledge about everything, such knowledge would fall under this precept (1699–1702).

19. A Precept of Father Visitor Andrés Luque: He set down the precept that no one could indebt himself beyond 100 pesos. Because he states "as a private person," some have interpreted this to mean that as a missionary or an administrator of the goods of a mission, this prohibition does not apply even if they exceeded 1000 pesos indebtedness. But Fathers Provincial Luis del Canto, Arteaga, and Salvatierra[46] all gravely prohibited this for missionaries, even holding that no superior could give permission to exceed 100 pesos indebtedness except in necessity and when the mission actually had enough to repay the debt in case the missionary died or was transferred.

20. A Precept of Father General Thyrso González: He first ordered that missionaries could not give over 50 pesos in alms; then he restricted this

---

[46] Juan María Salvatierra, S.J., born 1648 in Milan, entered the Society in 1668, and made his profession in 1684. He served in many positions of responsibility including Visitor to the Missions, Master of Novices, and as Provincial from 1704–1706. He died on his return from the California missions in Guadalajara in 1717.

to 30 pesos. Father Visitor Luque cut this to 25; Father Provincial Rodero, to 12; and Father Provincial Romano,[47] to 6 pesos.

21. A Precept of Father Provincial Díaz: He ordered that no missionary could play games, even those which were permissible in our colleges, with externs nor among themselves while laymen were present.

22. A Precept of Father Visitor General Lucas Luis Alvarez: No one can negotiate or contract anything not concerning the mission, even under the title of bartering, all of which has to be understood according to the mind and feeling of Rule 22 of Father Hernando Cabrero.

23. No one can bargain with grains or similar things in order to sell them; this precept has been reconfirmed by many superiors.

24. No one can accept alms for Masses.

---

[47] Alejandro Romano, S.J., born 1664 in Naples, entered the Society in 1680, and made his profession in 1699. He served as Provincial from 1719–22. He is last mentioned as the Rector of the Casa Profesa in Mexico in 1724.

Precepts of Father Provincial
Alexandro Romano

1. No Father or Brother in the Province is to be sent, under any title whatsoever, any silver, or money from the King's alms, or anything else of value, except medicines (which do not include bezoar stones), without written permission of Father Provincial which permission has to be prior to remittal.

2. No one can give anything of value worth more than six pesos to any person on the mission either as a token of gratitude or as alms without permission from the Visitor; if it would be to someone outside the Visitor's jurisdiction, then written permission from the Provincial is required and this permission must precede the remittal. If the case is urgent, permission can come from the Visitor.

3. No one will ship anything, whether by muledrivers or by someone else either in his own or a fictitious name, without permission of the Visitor, i.e. exclusive of the amount and outside the purposes of the shipment itself. The Visitor, under the same precept, will render an account to the Father Provincial at his first opportunity of who shipped how much to whom and why.

4. Those permissions which the Visitor can or could give in urgent cases can also be given by the Father Rector, but under the precept that he will notify the Visitor of what was done and why.

5. Whoever travels to Mexico will take only what is permitted. He will be allowed to give one mule to each servant and the rest he will entrust to Father Provincial.

6. No superior can give permission to remove more than what has been set down, but in the case of illness the Visitor of the Province can judge otherwise.

NOTE: They say Precept #7 was revoked by Father General Noyelle.[48] Precepts 12, 13, and 14 of Father Altamirano are also said to have been revoked. They say the same is true of 3 and 4. Concerning the precepts of Father Romano consult the end of the attached declaration. (Below)

---

[48] Carlos Noyelle, S.J., born in 1615, was the Praepositus General of the Society from 1682–86.

A Copy of a Letter by Father Provincial Juan Antonio Oviedo[49]

1. I revoke the precept of Father Provincial Romano that the missionaries cannot remit silver for furnishings and their needs except to the Province Procurator. I strictly order that although this might be useful to some of Ours, it is of no value for laymen [?].

2. Regarding the precept of the same Father Romano that our missionaries cannot give anyone within the Province anything that values 20 pesos, I declare that this is to be understood of the goods of the mission, but not in regard to the goods of the missionary himself which he has acquired as donations or gifts with the permission of superiors.

3. Regarding the precept of the same Father Romano that missionaries will not give relatives or friends any silver, not even as an alms, or anything else from the missions, even bezoar stones, I am limiting this so that once a year with the permission of superiors they can send up to 50 pesos; and I revoke that part which pertains to bezoar stones and other things which are found in the missions, such as napkins, trinkets, etc., with which they can regale their relatives and friends.

4. In order to clarify the precepts, I declare that when a Bishop, Governor or presidial commander comes to a mission, the missionaries can supply them with mules or similar things, but I am leaving in force the precept that they are not to be given any silver as a present unless it is a very extraordinary case.

5. Regarding the precept of Father Provincial Rodero that beggars and almoners cannot be given more than 12 pesos, I am restricting this to 6 pesos unless an authority, a special recommendation or an urgent circumstance might demand the sum to be increased to 12 pesos.

6. Regarding the precept of Father Provincial Luis del Canto that our missionaries cannot have brothers or relatives in their districts, I am restricting to mean, as residents; they can be received as guests as long as they are not women, and they can be helped and assisted like any other neighbor or traveller.

7. The receipt of stipends for Masses is a serious matter in the Society. I order that stipends are not to be accepted from Indians or Spaniards. If they insist, they will be accepted as stipends for some outsider to say the Masses, which will be explained to those giving the stipends.

8. The Father Visitor, when he does not find any inconvenience, can give permission for the Fathers to retain a mulatto or Spanish mestizo under the pretext of a mayordomo or similar office.

---

[49] Juan Antonio Oviedo, S.J., born 1670 in Santa Fé, Bogota, entered the Society in 1690, and made his profession in 1704. He served as Provincial from 1729–32; he died in Mexico City, April 2, 1757.

Remarks of an
Unknown Father Visitor,
About 1740

1. In regard to our privileges, the missionaries should not make use of them in order to issue dispensations in marriage without consulting either the Father Visitor or the immediate superior who is the Rector because many missionaries are unskilled in letters, etc.

2. The missionaries should not contract debts with laymen even if they need something for their own maintenance. Let the superior be of assistance by getting a loan from some nearby missionary. In this way the precept works no hardship.

3. When missionaries are en route from the Province to the mission, they should not divert themselves from the main road to visit other places. Since they have been given what they need for the trip, they should not ask loans of money from laymen which perhaps will never be repaid.

4. Those Fathers who have been deferred from taking final vows by the Provincial and the Consultors because of defects will not be allowed to remain in the missions. Rather, they will return to the colleges of the Province where they will undertake the correction of their faults and they will not return to the missions.

5. A subject who has been removed from the missions by the superiors from one of its provinces will not be detained by any superior in another province through which he passes on his way to the college of Guadiana or Guadalajara (whichever has been designated by the Visitor as his destination). The defects will be corrected only in the way prescribed; the subjects are not to be further punished.

6. When the visitors change a missionary, it should be to another mission of the same language in which he first ministered because if the language changes, no one will learn it. Knowing that the language to be used in the ministry is the same, they will apply themselves and perfect themselves in it.

7. I consider it very fitting that when a subject goes to the missions he should not be assigned to a mission right away. The superiors should put him at a mission where he can help out while he learns the language of the mission territory to which he will be assigned. Two or four men who know the language and who have been designated as examiners by the Provincial will test him. The examiners will be named by *informationes* sent to the Provincial and not by the choice of the examinee nor at his suggestion. These said examiners will also administer the examination that is required for profession.

8. It does not seem superfluous to me that, since the missionaries are obliged by charity or more strictly by their administration of the sacraments to the individuals of the mission territory who speak their own language, that all missionaries who have been on the missions for at least two years should be examined and approved by the said examiners as capable of ministry in the language. It seems that two years is enough because the Mexican Council stipulated only six months. This ruling would take effect only in case the preceding regulation had not been executed. If the subject has been examined and approved before entering the missions, it will not be necessary to examine him again.

9. It is well known that when the Indians do not talk with the Spaniards the Fathers learn the language. It is therefore prohibited for the Fathers to have a Spaniard in their company, except in the Tarahumara where the Indians are inclined to drunkenness or in recently converted missions because the missionaries have to talk with the Indians precisely in order to learn the language.

10. There are missionaries who most edifyingly go about their pueblos on a continual visitation. There are more who are careless. It is ordered that they assist equally as much in the pueblos of visitation as at the cabecera.

Precepts for the Missionaries Following the Decision of Father Provincial Andrés Xavier García[50] and His Consultors, June 25, 1747

1. Concerning the precept of Father Luis del Canto that Spaniards are not to be charged for interment, funerals, etc., unless they freely desire to give some payment, the precept is to be interpreted and understood in a way that does not permit more to be accepted from the parishioners, and not at all with the strictness of a fee. Whatever is so received will be entered in the ledgers and the money applied to the church.

2. Concerning the precept of Father General Thyrso González, which was confirmed by Father General Miguel Angel, that no costly buildings or valuable furnishing will be contracted for while the mission still has debts outstanding, and that if such furnishings were to be paid for by benefactors, the missionaries will not collect or utilize such donations except in very small sums — this precept is to be understood such that if some money is given for those purposes, it will be deposited in the power of some layman of trust and failing this, in power of the Father Rector of the district.

3. No one will play cards either with Ours or with externs. This precept extends to any of Ours betting, although only looking on at a card game being played by laymen.
will have any knowledge about the matter of mining, either directly or

4. No one will work mines. This includes the prohibition that no one indirectly. The intention of the precept is to include all forms of knowledge or interpretations that could even fall within the same precept.

5. The precept of Father Provincial Andrés Nieto[51] that anyone who has knowledge of anyone violating the precept against card-playing, whether with Ours or with externs, shall give notice to the Provincial, remains in effect.

6. The precept of Father Provincial Andrés Nieto that no one is to write the Viceroy, Bishops, or Governors without the permission of the Visitor and first sending him the letter, is extended to include the Oidores. And I, Father Provincial Andrés Xavier García, order that no missionary is to give certification to any extern whether in his favor or not.

---

[50] Andrés García, S.J., born 1686 in Estremadura, Spain, entered the Society in 1705, and made his profession in 1720. He served as Provincial from 1747–50. The last mention of him is as the spiritual director of the College of San Gregorio, Mexico, in 1764.

[51] Andrés Nieto, S.J., born 1660 in Toledo, Spain, entered the Society in 1675, and made his profession in 1696. He served as Provincial from 1726–29; he died in Mexico, December 26, 1750.

7. The precept of Father Luis del Canto remains in effect that the Fathers will not have any brother or other relative in their district, nor will they receive any relative into their houses except that he be treated like any other layman; nor will the Fathers give them anything either directly or indirectly; nor will they entrust anything to them; nor will the Fathers send either directly or indirectly any Indian to work in a mine or as a servant; nor will the Fathers favor their relatives by extending credit to merchants or any other persons involved in buying and selling clothing or anything else; nor will they remit or dispose of anything either directly or indirectly that touches on the support of their persons, houses or haciendas.

8. The precept of Father General remains in effect that neither educated women or Indian women will live inside the houses of the missionaries.

9. The precept of Father Provincial Gaspar Rodero remains in effect that no one will ask or accept anything from a layman in order to sell it.

10. Father Visitor Andrés Luque set down this precept: No one can indebt himself beyond 200 pesos [sic] with laymen; because he states "as a private person," some have interpreted this to mean that as a missionary or an administrator of the goods of a mission, this prohibition does not apply even if they exceeded 1000 pesos indebtedness; but Fathers Provincial Luis del Canto, Arteaga, and Salvatierra all gravely prohibited this for missionaries, even holding that no superior could give permission to exceed 100 pesos indebtedness except in necessity and when the mission actually had enough to repay the debt in case the missionary died or was transferred.

11. Father General Thyrso González first ordered that missionaries could not give over 50 pesos in alms; he then restricted this to 30 pesos. Father Visitor Luque cut this to 25; Father Provincial Rodero to 12, and Father Provincial Romano to 6. Father Provincial Andrés García is leaving the precept this way that the beggars are not to be given more than 6 pesos and this concession is precisely so they will move on.

12. No one will levy a stipend for Mass. This precept remains and it is to be understood that stipends for Masses will not be accepted except from the parishioners themselves and they will have to excuse themselves from receiving any others. Whatever they receive will be applied to the church as I have said about the other donations.

13. The precept that has been placed on the missionaries concerning the supplies that they ought to take and have with them when they change missions or return to the Province is hereby confirmed.

Additions by Father Provincial Andrés Xavier García

1a. No one shall send any silver to any laymen in Mexico, but only to the Procurator of the Province or some one of Ours for the supply of the missions. If anyone should violate this regulation, the Father Visitor is obliged to punish him by imposing a precept.

2a. All shall have a ledger of income and expense. The money received from grains will be registered in it, and they will list separately the income from cows, sheep, horses, mules, etc. They will also record expenses.

3a. If an Indian is to be punished for an ordinary fault, he will not receive more than 6 lashes. A more serious fault, 12; and the most serious, 25. In case they are women, never more than 8 and always at the hands of the governor or fiscal.

4a. No one is to make *entradas* into pagan lands without the permission of the Father Visitor, who will not give the permission without the opinion of the consultors.

5a. Let all take care to say a second Mass in the pueblos of visitation when they are a moderate distance away.

6a. Let everyone be in agreement about the grave obligation that each has by divine law of residing in the missions. Let all take care to fulfill this obligation and they shall not absent themselves from the missions except for very brief and set periods. For this reason Father Provincial strictly orders that no more than three Fathers will gather together for the profession of others and much less for other occasions.

Precepts of
Father Francisco Zeballos, 1763[52]

Father Provincial Francisco Zeballos in a letter of October 13, 1763, ordered that when a Father is changed from one mission to another, he will not remove anything that is there without the express permission of the Father Visitor, or at least, if he happens to be very far away and could not reply to the request, the permission of the Rector to whom the mission pertains.

In the same letter he also ordered that none of the missionaries will accept a deposit without the express permission of the Visitor or Rector, in the manner stated above; then he will note down in a fitting place which furnishings were deposited and to whom they belong.

It has been ordered several times and most recently by Father Provincial Zeballos that the oldest missionaries who have worked on the other missions are to be entrusted with the more comfortable missions, if they are vacant. This was set down in a letter of the said Father Provincial on April 1, 1764.

---

[52] Francisco Ceballos, S.J., born 1704 in Oaxaca, entered the Society in 1720, and made his profession in 1739. He served as Provincial from 1763–66; he was exiled in 1767 and died in Bologna, Italy, February 27, 1770. Although in this correspondence the name is spelled Zeballos, through history the correct spelling has been recognized as Ceballos.

Source Abbreviations

Selected Bibliography

Index

Source Abbreviations

AGI — Archivo General de Indias, Casa Lonja, Sevilla, Spain.

AGN — Archivo General de la Nación, Palacio Nacional, Mexico City.

AHH — Archivo Histórico de Hacienda, Palacio Nacional, Mexico City.

AHN — Archivo Histórico Nacional, Madrid.

AHP — Archivo del Hidalgo del Parral, Hidalgo del Parral, Chihuahua, Mexico.

APM — Archivo de la Provincia de México, Instituto Libre de Filosofía y Ciencia, Río Hondo, Mexico City.

ARSJ — Archivum Romanum Societatis Jesu, Jesuit Curia, Borgo Santo Spirito, Rome.

BL — Bancroft Library Manuscripts, The Bancroft Library, University of California, Berkeley.

BNM — Biblioteca Nacional de México, Archivo Franciscano and Manuscript Collections, Biblioteca Nacional, Mexico City.

BNS — Biblioteca Nacional de España, Manuscript Collection, Madrid.

BP — The Herbert E. Bolton Papers, the Bancroft Library, University of California, Berkeley.

WBS — The W. B. Stevens Collection, the University of Texas Library, Austin.

Selected Bibliography

Principal Archives

Archivo General de Indias, Casa Lonja. Sevilla, Spain.

Archivo General de la Nación. Palacio Nacional. Mexico City, Mexico.

Archivo Histórico de Hacienda. Palacio Nacional. Mexico City, Mexico.

Archivo Histórico Nacional. Madrid, Spain.

Archivo del Hidalgo del Parral. Hidalgo del Parral, Chihuahua, Mexico.

Archivo de la Provincia de México. Instituto Libre de Filosofia y Ciencia, Río Hondo. Mexico City, Mexico.

Archivum Romanum Societatis Jesu. Jesuit Curia, Borgo Santo Spirito, Rome, Italy.

Bancroft Library Manuscripts. The Bancroft Library, University of California. Berkeley, California.

Biblioteca Nacional de México. Archivo Franciscano and Manuscript Collections. Biblioteca Nacional. Mexico City, Mexico.

Biblioteca Nacional de España. Manuscript Collection. Madrid, Spain.

The Charles E. Beineke Collection. The Yale University Library. New Haven, Connecticut.

The Mariano Cuevas Collection. Instituto Libre de Filosofia y Ciencia, Río Hondo. Mexico City, Mexico.

The Herbert E. Bolton Papers. The Bancroft Library, University of California. Berkeley, California.

The Mateu Collection. Private collection of the Mateu family. Barcelona, Spain.

The Pablo Pastells Collection on New Spain and Hispanic America. Jesuit Research Library, *Razón y Fe* Institute. Madrid, Spain.

The Pablo Pastells Collection on the Philippines and the Marianas Islands. Jesuit Theologate Library, Saint Francis Xavier College. Barcelona, Spain.

The W. B. Stevens Collection. The University of Texas Library. Austin, Texas.

The University of Arizona Special Collections. The University of Arizona Library. Tucson, Arizona.

The Vatican Library Microfilm Collection. Pius XII Memorial Library, Saint Louis University. St. Louis, Missouri.

Printed Works — Books

Acosta, P. José de. *Historia natural y moral de las Indias*. Lima, Peru, 1583.

Alegre, P. Francisco Xavier. *Historia de la Provincia de la Campañía de Jesús de Nueva España*. Editors, Ernest J. Burrus and Felix Zubillaga. Rome: Jesuit Historical Institute, 1956–1960. 4 Vols.

Baegert, Jacob. *Nachrichten van der Amerikanischer Halbinsel Californien* Mannheim: 1773. Also in English, *Observations in Lower California*. Berkeley: University of California Press, 1952.

Bailey, Helen Miller, and Abraham P. Nasatir. *Latin America: The Development of Its Civilization*. New Jersey: Prentice Hall, 1968.

Bancroft, Hubert Howe. *History of the North Mexican States and Texas*. San Francisco: The History Company, 1884. 2 Vols.

Bannon, John Francis. *Missionary Frontier in Sonora, 1620–1687*. New York: U. S. Catholic Historical Society, 1955.

Bolton, Herbert Eugene. *Kino's Historical Memoir of the Pimería Alta*. Berkeley: University of California Press, 1948. Two volumes in one.

_____. *The Rim of Christendom: A Biography of Eusebio Francisco Kino, Pacific Coast Pioneer*. New York: The Macmillan Company, 1936. Reprinted, New York: Russell and Russell, 1960.

Burrus, Ernest J. *Kino and Manje, Explorers of Sonora and Arizona*. Rome and St. Louis: Jesuit Historical Institute, 1971.

_____. Editor, *Misiones Norteñas Mexicana de la Compañía de Jesús, 1751–1757*. México: Antigua Librería Robledo de José Porrúa e Hijos, 1963.

Chevalier, Francois. Editor. *Instrucciones a los hermanos jesuitas administradores de haciendas*. México: Universidad Nacional Autónoma de México, 1950.

Decorme, P. Gerard. *La Obra de los Jesuitas Mexicanos*. México: Antigua Librería Robledo de José Porrúa e Hijos, 1941. 2 Vols.

Denzinger-Schonmetzer. *Enchiridion Symbolorum: Definitionum et Declarationum*. Rome: Herder, 1964.

Diffie, Bailey Wallys. *Latin American Civilization: Colonial Period*. New York: Octagon Books, 1967.

Dobyns, Henry F. *Pioneering Christians Among the Perishing Indians of Tucson*. Lima, Peru: Editorial Estudios Andinos, 1962.

Donohue, John Augustine. *After Kino: Jesuit Missions in Northwestern New Spain, 1711–1767*. Rome and St. Louis: Jesuit Historical Institute, 1969.

Dunne, Peter Masten. *Andrés Pérez de Ribas*. New York: U.S. Catholic Historical Society, 1951.

_____. *Blackrobes in Lower California*. Berkeley: University of California Press, 1952.

_____. *Early Jesuit Missions in the Tarahumara*. Berkeley: University of California Press, 1948.

_____. *Pioneer Blackrobes on the West Coast*. Berkeley: University of California Press, 1940.

_____. *Pioneer Jesuits in Northern Mexico*. Berkeley: University of California Press, 1944.

Farriss, Nancy M. *Crown and Clergy in Colonial Mexico, 1759–1821: The Crisis of Ecclesiastical Privilege*. London: The University of London, Athlone Press, 1968.

Fúrlong Cardiff, Guillermo. *Missiones y sus pueblos de guaraníes*. Buenos Aires: Imprenta Balmes, 1962.

García, Luis Navarro. *Sonora y Sinaloa en el Siglo XVII*. Sevilla: Consejo Superior de Investigaciones Cientificas, 1967.

Gómez Hoyos, Raphael. *La Iglesia de America en Las Leyes de Indias*. Madrid: Instituto de Cultura Hispanica de Bogota, 1961.

Herring, Hubert Clinton. *History of Latin America from Beginnings to the Present*. New York: Alfred Knopf, 1961, revised 1968.

Hoffman, Ronan. *Pioneer Theories of Missiology*. Washington, D.C.: Catholic University of America, 1960.

Kino, Eusebio Francisco. *Favores Celestiales de Jesús y de María* SS^MA *y del Gloriosissimo Apostol de las Indias S. Francisco Xavier Experimentados en las Nuevas Conquistas y Nuevas Conversiones del Nuevo Reino de la Nueva Navarra.* Published as *Las Misiones de Sonora y Arizona.* Mexico: Archivo General de la Nación, 1922. Also published as *Kino's Memoirs of the Pimería Alta.* Herbert E. Bolton, translator. Berkeley: University of California Press, 1948.

_____. *Vida de Francisco Xavier Saeta.* Published as *Kino's Biography of Francisco Javier Saeta.* Translated with an Epilogue by Charles William Polzer; original Spanish text edited by Ernest J. Burrus. Rome and St. Louis: Jesuit Historical Institute, 1971.

Macero, Pablo. *Instrucciones para el manejo de las haciendas jesuitas del Perú.* Lima: Universidad Nacional Mayor de San Marcos, 1966.

Nentwig, Juan. *Rudo Ensayo.* San Agustín de Florida, 1863. Translated by Eusebio Guiteras and published in *Records of the American Catholic Historical Society of Philadelphia,* Volume V, June, 1894. Reprinted by Arizona Silhouettes, Tucson, 1951.

Och, Joseph. *Missionary in Sonora: Travel Reports of Joseph Och, S.J., 1755–1767.* San Francisco: California Historical Society, 1965.

Ortega, José, and Juan Antonio Balthasar. *Apostolicos Afanes de la Compañia de Jesús: Maravillosa Reducción y Conquista de la Provincia de San Joseph del Gran Nayar y Descubrimiento de los Padres Kino y Sedelmayer en la Pimería Alta.* Mexico: Editorial Layac, 1944.

Pérez de Ribas, P. Andrés. *Corónica y historia religiosa en la provincia de la Compañía de Jesús en Nueva España.* México: Sagrada Corazon, 1896.

_____. *Historia de los triunfos de nuestra Santa Fee entre gentes las mas barbaras y fieras del nuevo orbe.* Madrid, 1645. Translated and abridged by Tomás Robertson; published as *My Life Among the Savage Nations of New Spain.* Los Angeles: Ward Ritchie Press, 1968.

Pfefferkorn, Ignaz. *Description of Sonora.* Translated and edited by Theodore Treutlein. Albuquerque: University of New Mexico Press, 1949.

Polzer, Charles W., "Evolution of the Jesuit Mission System in Northwestern New Spain, 1600–1767." Ph.D. dissertation, University of Arizona, 1972.

_____. Translator and with an Epilogue, E. J. Burrus, editor Spanish text. *Kino's Biography of Francisco Javier Saeta.* Rome and St. Louis: Jesuit Historical Institute, 1971.

Ripalda, Geronimo de. *Catecismo Mexicano.* Edited by Ignacio de Parades, México, 1758.

Robertson, Tomás Antonio. Translator and editor. *My Life Among the Savage Nations of New Spain.* Los Angeles: Ward Ritchie Press, 1968. See Andrés Pérez de Ribas.

Shiels, William Eugene. *Gonzalo de Tápia, 1561–1594.* New York: U.S. Catholic Historical Society, 1934.

_____. *King and Church: The Rise and Fall of the Patronato Real.* Chicago: Loyola University Press, 1961.

Silva, Antonio da. *Trent's Impact on the Portuguese Patronage Missions.* Lisbon: Centro de Estudos Historicos Ultramarinos, 1969.

Spicer, Edward H. *Cycles of Conquest: The Impact of Spain, Mexico, and the United States on the Indians of the Southwest, 1533–1960.* Tucson: The University of Arizona Press, 1962.

Ulloa, Antonio de and Jorge Juan. *Voyage to South America.* London, 1806.

General References

Code of Canon Law of the Roman Catholic Church.

Documentos para la historia de México. Series IV. 21 Volumes.
    México: J. R. Navarro, 1853–1857.

Modern Spanish: A Project of the Modern Language Association.
    Modern Language Association. Introduction by William Riley Parker.
    New York: Harcourt, Brace, 1960.

Recopilación de Leyes de Indias. Impresión Quarta. Madrid: 1791. 3 Vols.

Regulae Societatis Jesu. Rome: Curia Praepositi Generalis, 1947.

Articles

Bolton, Herbert Eugene. "The Mission as a Frontier Institution in the
    Spanish-American Colonies." *American Historical Review,* Volume XXIII.
    October, 1917.

Burrus, Ernest J. "The Third Mexican Council in the Light of the
    Vatican Archives." *The Americas,* Volume XXIII. April, 1967.

Index